Nancy S. Arkin

Living and Working
in Paradise

Living and Working in Paradise

Why Housing Is Too Expensive and What Communities Can Do About It

William S. Hettinger

Thames River Publishing
Windham, Connecticut

Book cover and interior design by Pete Masterson, Æonix Publishing Group, www.aeonix.com. Body text set in 11 point Minion.
Cover photo by William S. Hettinger, Copyright ©2005.

Library of Congress Control Number: 2004107024

ISBN: 0-9755026-0-3

A statement from *The Geography of Housing* by Larry Bourne is quoted with the permission of the author.

Statements from "The Anatomy of Market Failure" by Francis M. Bator, reprinted in *The Theory of Market Failure: A Critical Examination,* are used with the permission of the Quarterly Journal of Economics.

Quotations from *The Economics of Welfare* by Arthur Pigou are used with the permission of Transaction Publishers.

Published by:
Thames River Publishing
PO Box 172
Windham, CT, 06280 USA

info@thamesriverpublishing.com

Printed in the United States of America

To all those struggling to find a decent and affordable place to live.

Contents

About the Author 11

Acknowledgments. 13

Introduction. 15

Part 1 Discoveries 19

1 Community Housing Choices 21

    Selection of Communities Studied 22

    Market Failure Analysis 23

    Housing Intervention 25

    Effect of Interventions. 26

    Programs. 27

    Summary of Research Findings. 30

    Revised Intervention Model. 30

2 The Community Evaluation and Intervention Process 33

    Community Evaluation 34

    Indicator Evaluation 34

    Evaluation Phase 35

        Housing Indicators 36

        Economic Indicators. 43

        Community Quality Indicators 46

        Demographic Indicators 47

        Macro and Micro Trends. 48

    Qualitative Evaluation 50

        Regulatory Constraints 50

        Topographic Constraints. 53

        Political Will 54

        Community Will. 55

    Housing Market Evaluation. 56

3 Community Intervention 59

    Creating a Housing Vision 59

Contents

Intervention Phase... 60
   Defining Housing Goals 62
   Analyzing Resources and Resource Gaps 63
   Identifying Necessary Actions 65
   Pinpointing Critical Success Factors 65
   Devising a Housing Intervention Plan 65
   Implementing Housing Interventions 67
4 Community Monitoring..................................... 69
   New Externalities 70
   Changes in Local Resources 70
Monitoring Phase.. 72
   Changes in Other Resources........................... 72
   Changes in Local Needs.............................. 72
   Diminished Intervention Effectiveness.................. 73
   Summary 74
5 Lessons For The Housing Practitioner 75
Critical Success Factors.................................... 75
   Political and Community Will 75
   Vision and Plan.................................... 76
   Buy-In 76
   Funding 77
   Land 78
   Organizational Capacity 78
Policy Implications 79

Part 2 Theoretical Foundations 83
6 Housing Market Economics.................................. 85
The Theory of Market Failure 85
   The Classical Argument.............................. 85
   The Case for Market Failure 86
Market Failure and Housing 89
   Regulatory Externalities 91
   Topographical Constraints 93
   The Second-Home Externality 94
Determining If Market Failure Exists 95
7 When Market Failure Occurs 99
Community Housing Crisis.................................. 99

Second-Home Demand 100
Land-Use and Zoning Regulations .101
Growth-Management Regulations. 102
Environmental and Topographical Constraints 104
Housing Intervention 104
Theory. 104
A History of Intervention 105
Housing and the Tourism Worker 107
The Need for Intervention 108

Part 3 Community Case Studies 109
8 Aspen, Colorado: A Pioneer in Resident Housing 111
Aspen Research 113
Tourism. 114
Housing Market Failure Analysis 116
Housing Market 116
Summary 120
Housing Intervention 120
Motivation for Intervention. 120
Effect of Intervention 121
Programs 123
Summary 124
Community Concerns 124
Summary of Research Findings. 126
9 Whistler, British Columbia: Planning for a Solution 129
Whistler Research 131
Tourism. 132
Housing Market Failure Analysis 133
Housing Market 134
Housing Intervention 138
Motivation for Intervention. 139
Effect of Intervention 140
Programs 142
Summary 144
Community Concerns 144
Summary of Research Findings. 146

Contents

10 Martha's Vineyard, Massachusetts: Leveraging Local Assets 149
    Martha's Vineyard Research 151
    Tourism 152
    Housing Market Failure Analysis 155
        Housing Market 155
        Summary 158
    Housing Intervention 159
        Motivation for Intervention 159
        Effect of Intervention 160
        Programs 161
        Summary 164
    Community Concerns 165
    Summary of Research Findings 166
11 Provincetown, Massachusetts: A Community at the Crossroads .. 167
    Provincetown Research 169
    Tourism 169
    Housing Market Failure Analysis 172
    Housing Market 172
    Summary 174
    Housing Intervention 176
        Motivation for Intervention 176
        Effect of Intervention 177
        Programs 178
        Summary 179
    Community Concerns 180
    Summary of Research Findings 181

Appendix: Research Method and Data Collection 183
    The Case Study Research Method 183
    Case Site Selection 185
    Data Techniques 187
    Data Analysis 189
Glossary 191
References 193
Index 201

Charts, Exhibits, and Tables

Chart – Community Evaluation and Intervention Process
    Evaluation Phase 35
    Intervention Phase. 60
    Monitoring Phase. 71
Chart – Growth-Management Regulations Imposed 103
Chart – Housing Indicators. 37
Chart – Housing Market Elasticity 100
Chart – Land-Use and Zoning Regulations Imposed 102
Chart – Second-Home Demand 101
Exhibit 1. – Revised Theoretical Model of Housing Market
    Intervention 31
Exhibit 2. - Theoretical Model of Housing Market Intervention. . . . 106
Table 1–1. Housing intervention programs 29
Table 2–1. Housing affordability in Martha's Vineyard. 41
Table 2–2. Employment by industry in Martha's Vineyard 44
Table 2–3. Average annual wages in Martha's Vineyard. 45
Table 8–1. Employment by industry in Aspen 115
Table 8–2. Housing affordability in Aspen 117
Table 8–3. Housing and population in Aspen. 122
Table 9–1. Employment by occupation in Whistler. 133
Table 9–2. Housing affordability in Whistler. 135
Table 9–3. Housing and population in Whistler 141
Table 10–1. Employment by industry in Martha's Vineyard. 153
Table 10–2. Housing affordability in Martha's Vineyard 156
Table 10–3. Housing and population in Martha's Vineyard. 161
Table 10–4. Affordable housing programs in Martha's Vineyard 163
Table 11–1. Business establishments in Provincetown 171
Table 11–2. Housing affordability in Provincetown 173
Table 11–3. Housing and population in Provincetown 177

About the Author

William S. Hettinger, Ph.D., is president and CEO of The Wyndham Financial Group, a consulting organization dedicated to helping communities design and implement housing and community development strategies, and evaluate the effectiveness of community development programs. His clients include Fortune 500 companies; national nonprofit organizations; and small, community-based nonprofits. Wyndham Financial is an industry leader in developing new and innovative approaches to community issues.

Hettinger has more than twenty years of experience in housing, real estate, and community development. Over the years, he has been a developer of affordable housing; a housing director; a mortgage broker; an asset manager; a portfolio manager; and a consultant to corporations and nonprofits engaged in real estate, community development, and performance evaluation.

He earned a Ph.D. in international development from the University of Southern Mississippi, where his research focused on housing and tourism. He also earned an MBA from Rensselaer Polytechnic Institute and a bachelor's degree from the University of Buffalo; and he is a graduate of the Economic Development Institute at the University of Oklahoma.

If you have questions or comments about the contents of this book, are seeking a speaker for your conference, or want to learn more about housing strategies and program evaluation, you can contact Bill Hettinger through The Wyndham Financial Group:

The Wyndham Financial Group, Ltd.
Phone   (860) 456–4477
Fax   (860) 456–1323
E-mail   billhettinger@wyndhamfinancial.com
Web site www.wyndhamfinancial.com

Acknowledgments

Writing a book is often a long and tedious process, with much time spent alone analyzing data, organizing thoughts, and then putting these thoughts on paper. But creating and publishing a book, particularly one like this that requires significant research, is far from a solitary task. Many people have been involved along the way, and their assistance and guidance has proved invaluable to me throughout the process. Because some of the research presented here was originally collected and published as part of the research for my Ph.D., I will start by thanking the members of my dissertation committee for their input and guidance: Dr. David Butler, head of the International Development Program at the University of Southern Mississippi and chair of my dissertation committee; Dr. Mark Miller and Dr. Clifton "Skeeter" Dixon of the University of Southern Mississippi; Dr. Jackie Haley; and Dr. Jack Phillips, who, in addition to serving on my committee, convinced me that this work needed wider distribution in the form of a book.

In addition, thank you to all those people in Aspen, Martha's Vineyard, Provincetown, and Whistler who answered my phone calls and e-mails and who graciously allowed me to interview them as part of this research. While I have agreed not to identify any of you by name, please know that I am greatly in your debt.

Thank you also to my editor, Lisa A. Smith, for her efforts on this project and to Pete Masterson, who, in addition to providing design and layout for the book, offered invaluable guidance during the publishing process.

Finally, I thank my family for their support. Thanks to my wife, Ann-Marie, for providing another set of eyes and proofreading the manuscript, and a special thanks to her and to my children, Laura and Jessica, for putting up with me during this project.

William S. Hettinger

June 2004

Introduction

In my twenty-five years of living in New England, it seems that every summer a Sunday edition of one or another of the local newspapers features an article about how expensive housing has become on Cape Cod or in some other tourism spot in the region. At first the articles featured local college students who had gone off for a planned summer of work and fun at the beach, enjoying the summer and earning enough money to continue their studies in the fall. The typical article would quote interviews with these seasonal workers, telling of how difficult it was to find housing and how expensive the housing was once they found it. They might have had to resort to sharing a house with many others who had also come for the summer, or they might have found an available bedroom in the home of a local resident.

Of late, the articles have become a bit more depressing. The stories, which at first featured college students who had to hustle a bit to find housing for the summer, have started to tell of much greater difficulties in finding housing and of much greater expense for the housing when it was found. One article a few years ago had a picture of the back basement entrance to the local supermarket and described people living in this space: a basement with beds and temporary walls, without adequate kitchen and bath facilities. The stories now tell of seasonal workers coming to town expecting to work a bit, have some fun, and save some money, but finding instead that they must work a lot simply to cover expenses, leaving little time for fun and little savings at the end of the summer. And the stories now quote interviews with the owners of the local hotels and restaurants, describing how important customer service is to their business and how difficult it has become to provide good service, or any service, because it has become so difficult to find a decent supply of workers. Housing costs have dried up the supply.

And more recently, articles have begun to appear detailing how difficult it has become even for middle-class families to find housing they can afford. The articles are not about the summer workers but about the year-round workers: teachers, medical professionals, civil servants, construction workers, and shop owners. The articles are about the people who form the backbone of the community, serving on town committees, volunteering with the PTA or Little League, voting in local elections; the people who know their neighbors and are willing to lend a helping hand. There is usually a discussion of how high and fast housing prices and rents have risen, and how difficult it is for those who are not independently wealthy to afford to live in the community. As the existing families retire or move away, the high housing costs make it difficult if not impossible for similar middle- and working-class families to move in; instead, the housing is sold to those who are more affluent.

Several years ago, I was invited to speak at "Preserving Community: Housing Our Island Families," a community conference on Martha's Vineyard to discuss the island's housing crisis. The meeting was to be held at a grange hall in one of the island towns. As we prepared for the meeting the night before, someone raised the question about what we would do if the number of people who wanted to attend exceeded the capacity of the grange hall. For fire safety reasons, the decision was made to close the doors when the legal capacity of the room was reached.

The next morning, when I arrived at the meeting site, I saw what I thought was a very large room. My first reaction was that I had never been to a housing meeting that had filled a room this size, and I thought there was no way we would fill this room. As it turned out, the room was full, and some late arrivals had to be turned away.

Audience members painted a picture of a community in crisis. The demand for housing had become so great that housing prices were rising rapidly; long-time residents were cashing in their houses and moving off island. The purchasers of the houses were wealthy people from off island, many of them summer residents who would not live in the community year-round and contribute to the local economy and the local community. It was becoming difficult to find workers for local businesses. Those who wanted to live on the island were unable to find affordable year-round housing. Several local residents were near tears as they described their fear of being forced from a community they could no longer afford to live in.

From this meeting, two clear themes emerged: housing had become a very expensive commodity, so expensive that it was about to destroy the core of the community; and the community was searching for a solution to the housing crisis that had developed.

As a researcher, I quickly translated the issues presented at the conference and in the summer newspaper articles into a series of research questions. What was happening to the housing economy on Martha's Vineyard? Was the market functioning efficiently or were external factors causing the market to run inefficiently?

According to economic theory, when external factors or externalities exist, the market can fail to function efficiently and a market failure can result. Was the housing market on Martha's Vineyard experiencing market failure? Were the other tourism communities on Cape Cod and throughout New England also experiencing market failure? Could housing market failure also be found in other tourism communities in the United States or in other parts of the world?

Had some tourism communities experienced housing market failure but reacted and intervened to correct the failure? Why did these communities intervene when others did not?

If there were communities that had intervened and worked to correct their housing market failure, how did they do it? What steps did they take? What programs did they use? What lessons did they learn along the way? Can these lessons be transferred and applied to housing interventions in other communities?

In an effort to answer these questions, I began reviewing the housing markets in more than twenty tourism communities worldwide. I examined such diverse places as Cape Cod; Orlando, Florida; the mountain resort communities of Colorado; Key West, Florida; Hilton Head Island, South Carolina; the Lake District of England; St. Andrews, New Brunswick, Canada; Cancun City and Puerto Adventuras in Mexico's Mayan Riviera; and the developing tourism destination Bays of Huatulco in the state of Oaxaca on Mexico's west coast.

In the end, I identified four communities for in-depth study: Aspen, Colorado, a world-famous winter and summer resort community in the Rocky Mountains, which had achieved a reputation as a community active in providing affordable housing for local residents; Whistler, British Columbia, Canada, a growing winter sports community in the mountains north of Vancouver, which in large part had used a master plan to guide its development and to provide housing for its residents; the island of Martha's Vineyard, off the coast of Cape Cod in southeastern Massachusetts; and Provincetown, Massachusetts, a summer artists and lifestyle community at the tip of the Cape Cod peninsula, with the largest difference between income levels and housing costs in the state.

I initially studied these communities in the summer and fall of 2002, as part of the research for my Ph.D. dissertation, *Living and Working in Paradise: Housing Strategies for Tourism Communities*. Some of the material in this book, including the case studies, was previously published in the dissertation, although much of it has been rewritten to appeal to readers in general.

For the book, I turned the dissertation upside down, putting my conclusions or discoveries first because I think they are of greatest interest to people who want to learn about how to fix problems in their own communities.

If you have a strong interest in economics or research, you may want to start with Part 2, which provides the theoretical foundation of my research, with information on the economic theory of market failure and community intervention.

If you have recognized that your community has housing affordability problems, you may wish to begin with Part 3, which present the case studies, so that you can compare your community with those on which my conclusions are based. Each of the case study chapters repeats the basic ideas to aid in understanding.

Or you may want to start by scanning the glossary, which defines the key terms used in the book. Wherever you begin, feel free to flip back and forth. In spite of what many people have been taught traditionally, there is really no rule that says you have to read the chapters of a book in order.

Part 1
Discoveries

1

Community Housing Choices

The study of four tourism communities at various stages of housing crisis and intervention forms the basis of the arguments and conclusions presented in this book. Aspen developed as a tourism community more than forty years ago, recognized early on that housing affordability was a problem, and established programs that now house approximately 64 percent of the town's population. The founders of Whistler studied Aspen and other resort communities, concluded that housing for local residents was an important component of a successful resort community, and included significant numbers of affordable housing units in the master plan for the community. Martha's Vineyard has experienced an explosion in popularity in the last fifteen years, with a developing housing crisis, significant worker shortages, and loss of community. The community has reacted by recognizing the developing crisis and beginning a process of leveraging local assets to create housing for community members. Provincetown has seen rapid growth in housing prices in the last decade and has experienced a significant increase in the number of second homes in the community. By 2002, when I conducted my research, the community was at a crossroads: it was experiencing a community crisis, and it needed to decide whether to intervene or not.

This chapter presents an overview of findings in the four communities by combining the results of the four case studies. The use of multiple cases in case study research can lead to the analytic generalization of case study results. In multiple case study research, the results of the individual cases are analyzed to build a general explanation (an analytic generalization) for the observed events, within the context of existing theory (Yin 1994). In this research, analytic generalizations have been built from the individual cases using the explanation-building analysis technique, an iterative data analysis technique in which the evidence from each case is analyzed individually and then continually compared to the evidence from the other cases to build a general explanation for the observed events. In using the explanation-building technique, a series of initial propositions regarding expected events are developed from the theory; these propositions are compared to observed events, and continually revised as the case study evidence is analyzed.

Selection of Communities Studied

At the outset of my research, I established conditions regarding the case sites to be studied: the communities needed to be established tourism communities, with tourism a key part of the local economy, and the communities needed to be geographically or otherwise discrete. Data for the individual case sites demonstrated that these conditions were met: 46.2 percent of the employment in Aspen related to tourism, more than 2.6 times the Colorado average; 38.4 percent of employees in Whistler worked in tourism, 50 percent more than the British Columbia average; 21.8 percent of employees on Martha's Vineyard were in tourism, 2.4 times the Massachusetts average; and 34.5 percent of the businesses in Provincetown were tourism related, 2.5 times the Massachusetts average.

Additionally, the four communities are geographically discrete, have topographic features that define them, and have limited overlap with surrounding communities. In each community, the workers' capacity to commute from adjoining communities is limited, and there is thus a need to house workers locally. Aspen and Whistler both are surrounded by mountains and accessible only by a single road; Martha's Vineyard is an island, primarily accessible by water; and Provincetown is at the end of a cape, with only a single road leading to it.

Preliminary evidence for Aspen, Whistler, and Martha's Vineyard indicated that community intervention in the housing market had taken place, and therefore they are referred to as positive case sites; although

Provincetown met the other criteria, preliminary evidence indicated that community intervention in the housing market had not taken place, and therefore it is referred to as the negative case site.

Market Failure Analysis

Part 2 of this book describes the theoretical model of housing market intervention (and see Exhibit 2 on page 106). The key premise of the model as applied to tourism markets is that when externalities exist in the housing market, supply and demand become unbalanced, leading to market failure in the form of unaffordable housing costs and displaced local residents. The three primary types of externalities are (1) topographical constraints; (2) growth-management, land-use, and zoning regulations, which primarily alter the supply side of the equation; and (3) second-home demand, which alters the demand side of the equation (Shucksmith 1981; Katz and Rosen 1987; Rose 1989; Mills 1995; Malpezzi and Green 1996; Pendall 2000; Gallent and Tewdwr-Jones 2001; Nelson et al. 2002). If these externalities exist in a tourism community, then conditions exist for market failure, and high housing costs and displaced local residents can be expected.

The data indicate that market failure has occurred in the communities studied. In each of the U.S. communities, a median-income family does not have sufficient income to afford a median-priced house; and in the Canadian community, a family with average income cannot afford an average-priced house. In contrast, a median- or average-priced house is affordable to comparable families in each state or province, and nationally in both countries. In each of the four communities, housing affordability, as indicated by the ratio of house prices to household income, is lower than housing affordability in the comparable state, province, or nation. Additionally, the interview data indicate that housing is unaffordable in the communities, with little or no free-market housing that can be purchased or rented by community residents.

Each community has topographical constraints and has imposed regulations that limit the supply of housing. In each community, geographic and environmental factors limited the supply of land that could be developed. And each community had imposed growth-management regulations designed to limit development, and land-use and zoning regulations that restricted the type and character of the housing developed.

Two factors influence the demand for housing in a tourism community: the number of local residents seeking housing and the number of second-home buyers seeking housing. Interviewees in the four communities identified second-home demand as having the biggest impact on the supply of housing available for tourism workers and community residents, and as having led to increased housing prices. Existing free-market housing units are being purchased by wealthy second-home buyers from external economies, thereby removing housing units formerly occupied by tourism workers and community residents from the system. Wealthy second-home buyers compete with local residents to purchase the available housing units, ultimately bidding up the price of the units beyond what local residents can afford. The result is a shortage of housing in the community and the displacement of local residents.

In the process of applying the explanation-building technique to analyze housing demand in the four communities, I examined the proposition that an inflow of workers to support and service the tourists was responsible for the increased housing demand. Only Whistler continues to see a significant increase in the number of tourism workers, and that community's strategic plan, affordable housing programs, and impact-fee structure includes at least a partial provision for these increases. The Whistler plan calls for the peak number of workers to be reached simultaneously with the development of the final units in the community. The other communities are not experiencing growth in the number of tourism workers, indicating that the problem is not increased demand for housing by new workers but the removal of worker housing units from the system, which is creating a shortage of housing; this leads to the conclusion that the conversion of existing residential units to second homes caused the supply of housing available to tourism workers and community residents to shrink, followed by increased prices and displaced residents.

Housing market failure resulting from externalities was identified in each community studied. Consistent with prior empirical research, interviewees in each of the four communities identified second-home demand as the primary externality affecting housing costs; they also identified growth regulations and topographical constraints as externalities.

Housing Intervention

When market failure occurs, an intervention is necessary to correct the failure and to provide what the market has not provided. When market failure has occurred in a tourism community, housing prices increase until housing is unaffordable to local residents, a housing crisis occurs, and the local residents complain to the local government and to community leaders. At this point, the community may choose to act or it may choose not to act. If the community chooses not to act, no intervention takes place. But if the community chooses to act, a housing intervention does take place. Two types of interventions have been successful in providing housing for community residents: the direct public provision of affordable housing units; and the public enablement of affordable housing development, in which private entities react to public incentives and privately create affordable housing. Public efforts to control second-home growth generally do not succeed (Shucksmith 1981; Gallent and Tewdwr-Jones 2000 and 2001).

Three motivations for housing market intervention have been identified in my research: reaction to a housing crisis in the community; the proactive planning for housing to support community and to facilitate a supply of tourism workers; and reaction to higher level government mandates. The motivation for intervention is the characteristic that distinguishes between the positive and negative case site communities. As the case studies in Part 3 show, Aspen, Whistler, and Martha's Vineyard all intervened in the housing market in reaction to a housing crisis in the community, following the pattern of intervention indicated by the literature; but Provincetown's motivation for intervention was a higher level government mandate and was not in reaction to a community crisis. In the positive case site communities, as housing costs increased, housing became unaffordable, local residents began to be displaced, community members complained to the local government and community leaders, and the community chose to intervene in the housing market; but in the negative case site community, resident complaints of a housing crisis have been ignored.

In addition to intervening as proposed by the existing theory, both Aspen and Whistler proactively intervened in the housing market in an effort to create and preserve community and to create a local supply of workers for tourism businesses. As Aspen made the transition to a tourism economy, community leaders saw housing as an important community element, integrated housing into the institutions they established, and instilled a culture of social involvement into the community, providing the base for Aspen's current housing programs. Whistler studied other tourism communities, identified unaffordable housing as a potential result of tourism development, and included plans for resident-restricted housing units in its development plans. Interviewees in both Whistler and Aspen cited the importance of having affordable housing available to preserve service levels in a tourism economy as motivation for including housing in their community's plans. Proactive planning for affordable housing in a tourism community is an additional motivation for housing market intervention, beyond the current theory.

Provincetown's primary motivation for intervening in the housing market, a reaction to a state mandate that 10 percent of the housing units in the community be affordable, is the characteristic that distinguishes it as a negative case site in this research. The literature does not identify a mandate from a higher level of government as a motivation for intervention, and in fact, the Massachusetts mandate applies to all communities in the state, not just tourism communities. A housing market failure and community housing crisis occurred in Provincetown; and the community faced the choice of whether to react or not. Provincetown took no action in response to the housing crisis but simply reacted to external requirements.

Effect of Interventions

The interventions resulted in mixed effects. The research indicates that the housing interventions have been successful in Aspen, where 64 percent of residents live in affordable housing, and in Whistler, where 32 percent of residents live in affordable housing. In both communities, the affordable housing is thought to have preserved the base of the community by allowing individuals and families to continue to live there. Without the housing, most people would live in other communities, and Aspen and Whistler would exist only for second-home owners and other tourists. Additionally, in each of these communities, the existence of affordable housing was thought to have created a stable supply of local workers for the tourism businesses, thereby increasing service levels.

The housing interventions on Martha's Vineyard are newer and have had a smaller effect on the community. Martha's Vineyard's programs house only 2.5 percent of community residents, and as of 2002 were targeted to house only 4.9 percent of community residents, significantly less than the levels achieved by Aspen or Whistler. The key effect of Martha's Vineyard's housing interventions to date has been to raise public awareness of the housing market failure on the island so that housing programs can be funded and implemented. Except for the families who have directly benefited from the housing programs, the interventions have not had much effect on the community, which describes its housing interventions as "pre-successful."

Provincetown's affordable housing programs have been estimated to house 6.6 percent of the town's population; however, they are thought to be skewed toward special needs and housing for seniors, without sufficient emphasis on families and local workers. My research identified Provincetown's housing programs as having had little or no impact on the community.

Overall, the research data indicate that the housing programs were generally successful for those community residents who received affordable housing under the programs. But because of the phenomenon of free-market housing units being converted to second homes, there are still residents in the four communities who cannot find affordable housing. The extensive conversion of free-market housing units to second homes was not planned for when the affordable housing programs were developed, and housing program goals have been difficult to achieve and maintain. Second-home conversions have mitigated some of the success of the affordable housing programs, and even the positive case site communities, with an extensive number of existing affordable housing units, continue to be affected by those conversions. Success from the housing programs is relative and not static.

Programs

As stated earlier, the public provision of housing and the public enablement of housing are the primary types of housing interventions.

Table 1–1 presents a summary of the housing programs implemented in the four communities I studied. Aspen's housing interventions are the oldest, having begun almost thirty years ago. Aspen has developed affordable housing directly; has offered incentives under the growth-management and land-use regulations, such as expedited approval or greater density, to developers who provide affordable housing; and has required developers who remove existing housing to mitigate the effects by replacing the housing units. Whistler has relied primarily on its zoning and growth-management regulations to require developers to include affordable resident and worker housing when commercial or residential projects are developed. Developers who do not develop sufficient housing are required to pay an impact fee to the community, and the fee is then used for the public development of affordable housing. Martha's Vineyard has implemented a multitude of community-based private programs to increase the number of affordable units on the island. Significant are the rental subsidy program, which subsidizes the difference between the free-market rent and the family's ability to pay, and changes in zoning regulations to allow affordable housing to be constructed on undersized lots and to legalize existing in-law apartments and converted summer cottages as affordable housing. Provincetown has publicly constructed a limited number of affordable units and has reallocated unbuilt units under its growth cap for affordable housing development.

Each community has used a different technique to finance its affordable housing development. Aspen has instituted a real estate transfer tax and a sales tax to pay for its affordable housing, raising $4.5 million per year for housing development and program operation. These funds allow Aspen the flexibility to purchase land for housing development in the free market and to implement programs without using federal or state money, thereby avoiding the income caps associated with these programs. Impact fees generated a C$6.5 million housing fund for Whistler, which was used by the housing authority to build affordable units and fund the operations of the housing authority. As a planned development on publicly owned land, Whistler has been able to designate specific areas for affordable housing development and was able to have an affordable housing land bank designated by the provincial government before private development began. Martha's Vineyard is funding its initial housing programs with private donations, accessing the wealth of the island to assist in preserving its character. As in Aspen, the use of private funds in Martha's Vineyard exempts it from the income caps associated with federal and state programs. Public affordable housing development in Provincetown has relied on state and federal money.

Table 1-1. Housing intervention programs

	Aspen	Whistler	Martha's Vineyard	Provincetown
Direct public development				
Publicly owned or developed housing	✓	✓	✓	✓
Market purchase of housing units			✓	
Public enablement				
Requirement for affordable units under growth cap		✓		✓
Exemptions from growth cap quotas	✓	✓		
Greater density / re-laxed zoning regulations	✓	✓	✓	✓
Expedited approvals	✓			
Mitigation requirements	✓			
Rental subsidy			✓	
Conversion of existing units to affordable housing			✓	
Funding				
Impact fees		✓		
Real estate transfer tax	✓			
Sales tax	✓			
State and federal agencies				✓
Private donations			✓	
Affordability controls				
Deed restrictions	✓	✓	✓	✓
Resale price caps	✓	✓		

Each community uses deed restrictions to control unit occupancy and maintain affordability. Additionally, for ownership units, Whistler and Aspen set resale price caps to control the proceeds and profit owners can receive.

Summary of Research Findings

Externalities have been identified as a cause of market failure in housing markets. In each of the four communities studied, the externalities of second-home demand, topographical constraints, and growth-management and land-use and zoning regulations existed; and they have led to increased housing costs, unaffordable housing, and the displacement of local residents. A housing market failure has occurred in each of these communities. When market failure occurs, the community must choose whether or not to intervene to correct the failure. An intervention has been observed in each of the four communities, but their motivations for intervention differ. The literature cites reaction to a community crisis as the motivation for intervention, and according to my research, that motivation is present in the three positive case site communities. Additionally, my research identified the proactive intervention in housing, before a market failure occurs, as an additional motivation for intervention by two of the positive case site communities. This finding adds to the existing literature. Finally, my research identified the need to comply with higher level government regulations as a motivation for intervention in the negative case site community. Because this intervention is driven by a need to comply with an external requirement and not by a need or choice to correct a market failure, it is outside the scope of market failure theory.

Revised Intervention Model

The results of this multiple case research indicate that there are two motivations for tourism communities to chose to intervene in the housing market: a reaction to a market failure that has occurred; and, given the recognition that externalities will lead to market failure, proactive planning for housing.

On page 106, you will find Exhibit 2, which shows the classic theoretical model of housing market intervention. Here, in Exhibit 1, I present a revised theoretical model of housing market intervention. Below

Exhibit 1. – Revised Theoretical Model of Housing Market Intervention

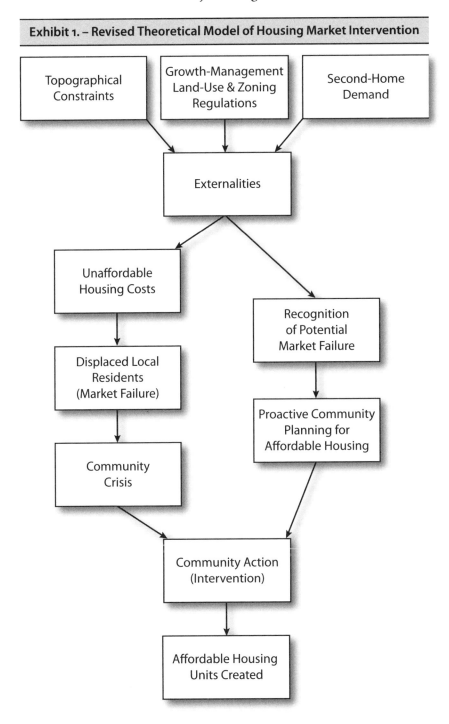

the externalities on the model, the left side shows the results named in the literature. The identified externalities lead to unaffordable housing costs, which lead to displaced local residents and market failure; the community chooses to react to a crisis, and intervenes to create or enable the creation of affordable housing units. The right side represents the motivations for intervention identified by my research. The community recognizes the existence or prospective existence of externalities that can lead to market failure, and rather than waiting for market failure to occur, it proactively plans for affordable housing units and acts to create them or to enable their creation.

2

The Community Evaluation
and Intervention Process

nalyses of the four communities individually (see Part 3) and as
a group (see chapter 1) has determined (1) the common factors
indicating that a housing market failure has occurred or is likely to occur, (2) the motivations for the interventions that have occurred,
and (3) the common and unique intervention strategies that have been
pursued.

As a result of these efforts, I have created the Community Evaluation
and Intervention Process™. This is a methodology for examining and evaluating the housing market in a community for the existence of market
failure or for the factors and conditions that have been shown to lead to
market failure, and for developing a vision, strategy, and plan for community intervention to address the market failure and provide housing
for community residents.

The Community Evaluation And Intervention Process
Community Evaluation
Indicator Evaluation
Qualitative Evaluation
Housing Market Valuation
Community Intervention
Community Monitoring

The Community Evaluation and Intervention Process is applicable not only to communities in which the economy depends heavily on tourism but to any community in which significant externalities affect the free functioning of the housing market. The Community Evaluation and Intervention Process should be used to evaluate any community in which (1) housing prices have risen faster than incomes, (2) housing has become unaffordable to local residents, or (3) the community is experiencing a housing crisis.

Here and in the following chapters, I present the processes for evaluating, intervening in, and monitoring a community. Housing practitioners can use this information as a how-to guide in the evaluation of a community's housing market and in the development of intervention strategies to deal with or prevent a community housing crisis.

Community Evaluation

The evaluation phase of the Community Evaluation and Intervention Process entails a careful and rigorous examination of the community and its housing market to ascertain whether the community is experiencing a housing crisis or is likely to experience a housing crisis, and to set the stage for future interventions or for adjustments in the current intervention process. From the evaluation of the community, a community vision can be created and intervention strategies developed and implemented.

Community evaluation involves the collection of quantitative and qualitative information about a community, the evaluation of this information, and an assessment of the community and the housing market, including a review of the community's housing, social, employment, economic, and demographic indicators, a review of regulatory constraints, a review of topographical constraints, the identification of macro and micro trends affecting the community, the assessment of the housing market and identification of key issues, and the evaluation of the community for current or prospective housing market failure.

Indicator Evaluation

The indicator evaluation involves a review of a community's numeric and statistical data, including indicators of housing, the economy, community participation, and demographics. Indicators paint a statistical

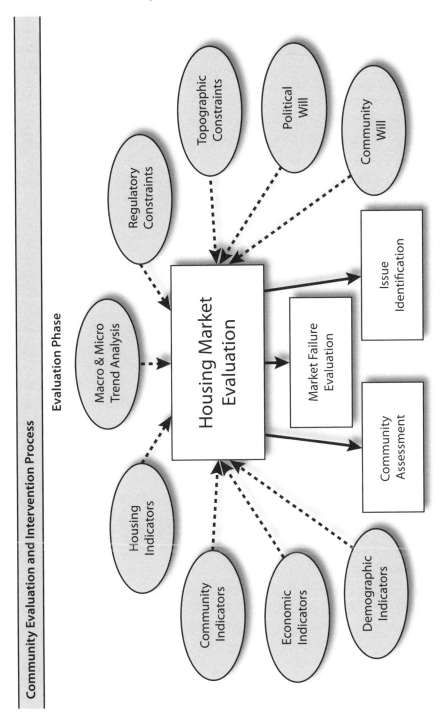

Community Evaluation and Intervention Process

Evaluation Phase

Topographic Constraints

Political Will

Community Will

Regulatory Constraints

Macro & Micro Trend Analysis

Housing Indicators

Housing Market Evaluation

Market Failure Evaluation

Issue Identification

Community Assessment

Community Indicators

Economic Indicators

Demographic Indicators

picture of the community that can be used (1) as a point of reference for assessing its current status; (2) to measure progress and the effectiveness of the housing interventions performed; and (3) for comparison with similar communities, with "typical" communities or national averages, and with dissimilar communities.

The indicator evaluation requires the collection and assessment of a community's quantitative data; reviewing existing data from local, regional, or national sources; and collecting community-specific data from sources within the community. The indicator data to be collected and reviewed include current data, historical data, and projections of future data.

A current debate among academics and community indicator practitioners revolves around how many indicators should be used to measure an event in a community. The academics tend to favor the use of many indicators, sometimes hundreds, along with statistical techniques or indexes to simplify and classify them. On the other hand, practitioners tend to rely on only a few indicators, sometimes missing trends and events that would have been identified with the use of a few more related indicators.

From a practical perspective, it is easier to use a smaller number of good indicators that measure the events of interest and the trends affecting those events than it is to use a large number of indicators measuring many events and then trying to simplify and combine them. The trick is making sure the indicators selected are good. Good indicators need to be identified and selected with care so that they can be used to measure the events of interest.

Housing Indicators

Let's start with housing indicators. The many indicators of housing and housing affordability in a community include the number of housing units; the number of housing units occupied by their owners; the number of units rented or available for rental; and the type of rental units, such as those in large apartment complexes, in multifamily homes, or in individual houses and apartments. Additional measures might include the size of the typical owner-occupied or rental unit, measured in square footage or number of bedrooms; the percentage of units that are typical; and the percentage of units that approach or exceed the typical size.

Housing Indicators

Data Indicators
    Population
    Number of households
    Average household size
    Number of housing units
    Type of housing units
      (Single family, multifamily, apartments, condos)
    Owner-occupied units
    Renter-occupied units
    Number of rental units
    Number of owned units
    Number of vacant units
    Number of second-home units
      (from the census, from tax bills, from school and voter records)
    Housing prices
      (range, median, average, distribution)
    Rental costs per unit or per bedroom
    Family income
      (range, median, average, distribution)
    Wage rates for hourly workers
    Wage rates based on types of work and hours worked
    New immigrant population estimates
      (including legal and illegal immigrant population)
    Population by income group
    Number of families paying more than 30 percent of income for housing
    Percent of families paying more than 30 percent of income for housing
    Number of families paying more than 35 percent of income for housing
    Percent of families paying more than 35 percent of income for housing

Calculated Indicators
    Ratio of housing costs to income
    Ratio of house prices to income
    Ratio of rent costs to income
    Affordability of home purchases for a family

Indicators of housing affordability typically include measures of the number or percentage of families paying more than 30 percent or 35 percent of their income for housing (the standard government measures of affordability). Affordability indicators also can include measures of the cost of homeownership or rental, such as homes purchase prices, apartment rents, mortgage costs, property taxes, and the money needed for a home purchase down payment; these measures, when combined with income indicators, can be used to develop an index of affordability.

The list below identifies the housing indicators that can be used to assess housing affordability and the overall housing market in a community.

The list shows two kinds of housing indicators: those in the form of raw data and those that can be calculated from the raw data. For example, population, housing prices, income, and number of second homes are raw data; the ratio of housing costs to income or the percentage of second homes as a percentage of total housing supply are calculated indicators. In general, calculated indicators will be more useful than raw data in the evaluation process, but the raw data will be needed to perform the calculations. The first step in using indicators to evaluate a community is to collect the data indicators (i.e., the raw data).

Data indicators typically can be acquired in one of two ways: from existing data banks that have been published by some government agency or other entity, or from original research performed as part of the evaluation process. In the United States, many of the data indicators listed above are collected every ten years during the census process. But not all government censuses are the same, occur with the same frequency, or include the same data. For instance, Statistics Canada conducts a census of Canadian communities every five years, but it does not include data on the number of second homes in a community and does not capture extensive data on the many smaller communities in Canada. The same is true for many of the censuses conducted in Europe; key data elements needed to effectively evaluate a housing market for market failure may be missing. In less developed countries, censuses may occur with differing frequencies, if at all, and many cover only highly populated areas, leaving out much of the countryside and the natural areas where tourism development is likely to occur.

When the data needed for the evaluation does not exist, is rapidly changing, or is stale, as is the case with the U.S. Census data as the end of the ten-year cycle nears, original data will need to be collected as part of the community assessment process. For example, in evaluating the housing market in Whistler for market failure, the number of second homes in the community was not available from Statistics Canada, so I estimated the number using bed-unit data collected by the community and triangulated to estimates provided by community officials.

Had I not been able to calculate second-home data from existing community data, or had the data been old, it would have been necessary to collect it directly from community records. One method for accomplishing this task is a detailed review of the mailing addresses on the property tax bills. Second-home owners by definition have a primary residence at another location and are likely to have listed their primary residence as the mailing address for the tax bill. By comparing properties whose owners have out-of-town mailing addresses with a list of property types to weed out apartments and other rental properties typically owned by out-of-towners, the estimated number of second homes in the community can be determined.

Income and population data not available from existing data indicators could be collected using surveys and other data collection methods, and analyzed using statistical methods to develop statistically accurate estimates. Other housing data such as unit sizes and number of bedrooms can be determined through a review of the development records or tax assessment records maintained by the local community.

The most important use of indicators is assessing the housing market in a community to determine whether housing is affordable to community residents and the local workforce. If most families cannot afford to live in the community, this is a good indication that the community is experiencing a housing market failure, with the existence of or potential for a community housing crisis.

The use of multiple indicators allows for the comparison and triangulation of the indicators to assess the housing market from several different perspectives, and limiting the overall number of indicators simplifies the analysis process and prevents the analysis from getting lost in statistical processes.

In evaluating the four communities for market failure, I emphasized several indicators: the percentage of housing units that were second homes; the ratio of house prices to household income; the ability of a median-income family to afford a median-priced house; and the percentage of households paying more than 30 percent of their income for housing.

In evaluating the housing market, the percentage-of-second-homes indicator can be used to assess the importance of second homes in the local housing market. Second homes were one of the externalities identified as a cause of housing market failure, so if the number of second homes is significant, a condition of market failure may exist.

As an example, consider the case of Martha's Vineyard presented in table 2–1.

In 2000, 53.6 percent of the housing units on Martha's Vineyard were second homes, and the percentage of second homes grew by more than 15 percent from ten years earlier. Additionally, the percentage of second homes in Martha's Vineyard is more than 16 times the national average. The evaluation of these indicators points to second homes as an important factor in the Martha's Vineyard housing market.

The ratio of house prices to household income and the ability of a median-income family to afford a median-priced house are the important indicators of housing affordability in a community. If community residents and local workers cannot afford housing, a community crisis is likely to result as local residents are displaced and new middle-class residents are unable to afford housing in the community.

The ratio of housing prices to household income measures the relative affordability of housing in a community. The existence of high housing prices alone does not mean a community is unaffordable. A problem begins to occur only when the housing prices are significantly above income levels; this indicator is designed to identify these instances.

The ability of a median-income family to afford a median-priced house is an indicator of who can afford to make the monthly mortgage payments on a home in the community. Stated differently, it is an indicator of whether a median-income family can qualify for a mortgage loan to purchase property from a traditional mortgage lender.

Again, using the example of Martha's Vineyard, we see that the ratio of housing prices to household income on Martha's Vineyard is more

Table 2–1. Housing affordability in Martha's Vineyard, Massachusetts, and the United States

	Martha's Vineyard		Massachusetts		United States	
	2000	1990	2000	1990	2000	1990
Housing units that are second homes	53.6%	46.4%	3.6%	3.7%	3.1%	3.0%
Median household income	$45,559	$31,994	$50,502	$36,952	$41,994	$30,056
Median house price	$304,000	$195,800	$185,700	$162,000	$119,000	$79,100
Ratio of house price to household income	6.7	6.1	3.7	4.4	2.8	2.6
Available funds monthly for housing at 30% median household income	$1,139	$800	$1,263	$924	$1,050	$751
Monthly cost for median-priced house	$1,823	$1,174	$1,113	$971	$713	$474
Excess income or (income gap)	($684)	($374)	$149	($47)	$336	$277
Households paying more than 30% of income for housing	31.8%	35.6%	27.8%	31.0%	26.9%	27.3%

Source: 1990 and 2000 United States Census.

than double the national average, indicating that incomes on the island have not kept pace with the increase in housing prices. We also see that a median-income family needs an income that is 60 percent greater in order to qualify for a traditional mortgage loan on a median-priced house. The evaluation of these two indicators points to a mismatch between income and housing costs, with the likely result that housing is unaffordable to the typical community resident and that a housing crisis either exists or will arise for those who need to purchase housing in the community.

A final indicator used to evaluate a community's housing market for market failure is the percentage of households or individual residents paying more than a certain percentage, usually 30 or 35 percent, of their income for housing. When households and individuals have to spend too much of their income for housing, they have too little income remaining for other purposes, such as food, transportation, clothes, and taxes; the United States Department of Housing and Urban Development (HUD) has established the 30-percent-of-income threshold as the dividing line between affordable and unaffordable housing. Other countries, including Canada and much of Europe, use a 35-percent threshold. At either threshold, this indicator presents a measurement standard that is readily comparable across communities worldwide.

In Martha's Vineyard and the other communities described in this book, the comparison of the percentage of households paying more than 30 percent of income for housing to the percentage in the region and nation shows that there are significant differences in housing affordability. For instance, Martha's Vineyard has 14 percent more households paying in excess of 30 percent of their income for housing than does the State of Massachusetts overall, indicating that housing is more unaffordable on Martha's Vineyard than in other places in the state.

When using this indicator to evaluate communities with a large concentration of low-wage workers such as those found in tourism communities, it is important to consider not only the families and households paying more than 30 percent of their income for housing but to consider housing costs relative to the income of individual low-wage workers, particularly when the workers do not live in traditional family settings but in dormitories or shared houses or apartments.

While the percentage of income that households or families pay for housing is typically collected with census data, the data on the housing costs of individuals may not be as readily available. In that case it may be necessary to use surveys and other research methods to collect the data needed for the indicators.

Economic Indicators

Local economic activity is often a key factor in defining the wages and salaries of the local workforce and has a direct effect on the ability of a family or individual to afford housing. Indicators of economic activity in a community include the number of employers; number of workers per employer; distribution of workers among small, medium, and large employers; employment by industry; and the relative wages of each worker group. In a tourism community, the mix of tourism-related employment and other employment is also important, as are the changes in employment and industries over the tourism seasons.

Additionally, characteristics of the workforce and community residents, such as age, education, and skill level, and information on the commute patterns of the local workers and community residents should also be obtained.

The primary source of economic and employment data in the United States is the Census Bureau, which conducts an economic and business census every five years, collecting community level data on employers and their employees. The economic census collects information on local businesses, aggregates the information, and produces results by industry group, at the zip code level. The information includes the number of business establishments, revenues, payroll, number of employees, and the distribution of employment by industry and business size. From this data, an economic profile of the community can be developed.

Table 2–2 (page 44) gives of an overview of employment by industry in Martha's Vineyard compared with Massachusetts and the United States overall.

As the indicators in table 2–2 show, Martha's Vineyard has more than twice the tourism employment as Massachusetts overall, and also has significantly more tourism-related employment in construction, real estate, and retail trade than is typical for Massachusetts or for the United States. Conversely, other non-tourism industries are underrepresented on the island. These indicators point to the importance of tourism in the island's economy.

Continuing with the Martha's Vineyard example, the housing

Table 2–2. Employment by industry in Martha's Vineyard, Massachusetts, and the United States (percent)

	Martha's Vineyard	Massachusetts	United States
Tourism employment			
Arts, entertainment & recreation	2.7	1.4	1.5
Accommodation & food services	19.1	7.7	10.2
Total tourism employment	21.8	9.1	11.7
Other employment			
Construction	15.0	4.0	5.8
Real estate & rental & leasing	2.8	1.5	1.7
Retail trade	20.7	11.4	13.0
Finance & insurance	5.0	7.0	5.2
Professional, scientific & technical	3.6	7.5	6.0
Other	31.2	59.4	56.6
Total other employment	78.2	90.9	88.3
Total Employment	100.0	100.0	100.0

Source: 2000 County Business Patterns, U.S. Census Bureau.

indicators discussed above showed that income levels and housing prices on Martha's Vineyard were mismatched, with its residents unable to afford the median housing on the island. Table 2–3 presents comparative data on the island's wages. The average wage data, developed by dividing the total annual payroll by the number of workers in that industry, shows average incomes in the $10,000 to $21,000 per year range for tourism workers, less than half the island's median family income. Even though tourism is a key part of Martha's Vineyard's economy, wages in tourism are lower than in other economic sectors.

Table 2–3. Average annual wages by industry in Martha's Vineyard and the United States (dollars)

	Martha's Vineyard & Cape Cod	United States
Tourism economy		
Arts, entertainment & recreation	21,447	20,651
Accommodation & food services	11,321	10,264
Tourism-related employment		
Construction	35,884	30,748
Real estate & rental & leasing	29,445	24,430

Source: 1997 Economic Census, U.S. Census Bureau.

In addition to the wage and industry data, the commute patterns of the local workers and residents should be considered. Are workers for local businesses imported each day from adjoining communities, or do local residents commute to other communities for their employment? Commute patterns affect housing demand. Commute-pattern data is available from the U.S. Census every ten years, and in the interim can be obtained through survey and other research techniques.

It is also important to identify and review trends that may be affecting the local economy, particularly those involving major employer industries that are either growing or contracting. This can be accomplished through a time-series analysis of the economic indicators discussed above, and more qualitatively through interviews and focus-group discussions with local officials and local business and community leaders.

Community Quality Indicators

Data can be collected and quantitative indicators developed to evaluate the quality and effectiveness of a community, and the participation in the community by those who live or own property there. Through the use of quality indicators, a community can evaluate the extent to which a common community (i.e., a common political, legal, and social structure) exists and can measure changes over time. As the housing market begins to fail in a community, a decline in its quality and attractiveness can be expected.

Community Quality Indicators

Civic Involvement
    Open, unfilled board positions
        Town boards
        Civic organizations
    Participation in volunteer organizations
        PTA, Little League

Economic Health
    Open positions in local businesses
        Tourism jobs
        Professional positions
    Open positions in key community services
        Teachers
        Town workers
        Police and Fire
        Health care

Indicators of community quality and effectiveness typically must be developed locally. There is no national database or census bureau collecting data on community effectiveness. Fortunately, much of the data needed for the development of these indicators is readily available from sources in a community. The data simply has to be collected.

Indicators can be constructed to measure the civic involvement of residents using data on the number of open, unfilled positions on the boards of community organizations. Indicators of volunteer involvement can be constructed using board and participation data from local volunteer organizations such as youth groups, sports leagues, and the PTA. A time series of these indicators can be used to evaluate the growth or decline of civic involvement among residents.

As the research results from several of the case studies described in this book indicate, when a community begins to experience housing market failure, the younger community residents, who typically make up the majority of civic and volunteer boards, begin to decline in number, and the community begins to experience a greater number of open board seats and available volunteer jobs.

Indicators of community quality can be constructed from a review of the employment openings in local businesses and a review of the reasons for departure of local employees who leave their jobs and move to other communities. The lack of affordable housing will affect local businesses—particularly retail, accommodation, and other low-wage industries—first, and these industries will experience high housing-related turnover and a significant number of open, unfilled positions. If the turnover or number of unfilled positions is significant in key jobs such as police, fire, teaching, or health care, then the community should develop indicators to evaluate whether the job turnover is related to housing. As the housing market begins to experience market failure, with housing becoming unaffordable to community residents, a community will have difficulty finding job applicants who are able to accept the available positions, and lack of affordable housing will be cited as a key reason. The result will be a community without adequate key community services, businesses without adequate service levels, business owners chained to their businesses because they cannot find help, and an overall decline in the quality of the community.

Demographic Indicators

The demographics of a community can also have an impact on housing affordability and the vitality of the local economy. Two important demographic areas should be evaluated: who the house buyers and sellers are, and how well the local population matches the workforce required by local businesses.

A community becomes at risk when long-time community members sell their houses, move out of the community, and are replaced by people who are not active in community life, such as second-home owners or retirees. Home buyer and seller data should be analyzed to identify trends affecting the local community. The trend analysis should include examination of the number of young people and young families moving to or from the community, and the number of retirees and future retirees, and whether they are moving away, staying, or moving into the community. Data for this evaluation can be obtained from local sources such as surveys of home buyers and sellers, surveys of local realtors with knowledge of the transactions, and municipal tax and school records.

In an ideal world, the education and skills required for the jobs available from local businesses would match the education and skills offered by local residents, and there would be a sufficient number of local residents available to fill the available jobs. But the world is not ideal, and a community becomes at risk when a mismatch develops between jobs and community members. Demographic indicators can be developed from quantitative data, such as age, income, education, and business requirements; and those indicators can be used to evaluate the employment supply and demand in a community.

My research identifies unaffordable housing as an instance in which this mismatch could occur. When housing is unaffordable, the community will begin to age. No young individuals or families will be able to afford housing in the community and hence will not move to it; and as time passes, the existing community residents will age and begin to retire. Those who buy housing in the community will be wealthier and will not be available to fill the lower wage jobs. In a tourism community, which has many low-wage jobs, a mismatch will develop between available jobs and available workers. An analysis of demographic indicators and trends would allow a community to evaluate and react to such a situation.

Macro and Micro Trends

An important tool that uses indicators to evaluate a community for existing or prospective housing market failure is a macro and micro trend analysis of the factors affecting the community and the indicators. The indicators present a historical and current picture of the community.

The trend analysis allows the community to project the picture into the future.

Some projections can be done with a high degree of certainty; others may be less certain and will require the evaluation of several alternative scenarios. For instance, in forecasting school enrollment, under normal circumstances it is possible to forecast with accuracy the number of fourth graders expected next year by simply looking at the number of third graders this year. It is also possible to forecast the number of fifty-year-olds in ten years by looking at the number of forty-year-olds today and adjusting for expected mortality. It would be less easy to make a five-year forecast of the number of twenty-five-year-olds living in a specific tourism community with unaffordable housing costs. Such a forecast might involve the analysis of several what-if scenarios.

A macro trend analysis identifies the state, national, and international trends affecting the community, while a micro trend analysis identifies the individual or local trends affecting the community. Trends should be analyzed for each of the housing, economic, community quality, and demographic indicators. Indicators should be projected into the future for one or more scenarios.

For example, consider some of the macro trends identified in my research. The post-World War II baby-boom generation, the largest population block in the United States and Western Europe, is aging, with many of its members at or rapidly approaching retirement age. The members of this baby-boom generation were identified as some of the primary buyers of second homes in the tourism communities I studied. The macro trend of an aging population, with accumulated wealth, is one of the driving factors affecting housing demand in tourism communities. Likewise, second homes were identified as an attractive investment alternative. The macro trend of low yields on bonds and declining stock market returns made real estate in general—and second homes in tourism communities in particular—a more attractive investment; this led to increased demand for second homes. A change in either of these macro trends would affect the demand for second homes in tourism communities.

As stated above, micro trends affect an individual community. In Aspen, for example, a significant number of baby boomers in their fifties live in the community's affordable housing and work locally. While the macro trends indicate that a significant percentage of retirees will move to other communities, making their housing available to replacement workers, a micro trend appears to be occurring in Aspen, which expects a smaller percentage of retirees to move because of the attractiveness of their existing living arrangements and lack of housing equity. The micro demographics of Aspen are changing differently from the macro demographics of the country.

Macro trends that should be analyzed include the returns available from investments other than real estate; foreign exchange rates, particularly if the community relies on foreign second-home buyers or foreign tourists; demographics; and tourism trends. Micro trends that should be analyzed include the demographics of the local community, the relative attractiveness of the community's tourism product compared with alternatives, and the relationship of housing supply to housing demand.

When the effect of micro and macro trends is not readily apparent, a multi-scenario what-if analysis of the community should be conducted with varying micro trend assumptions to determine their likely effects on the community's housing market. When used effectively, the trend analysis and what-if scenario analysis may assist a community in identifying prospective instances in which housing market failure will occur and instances in which it would not be expected to occur.

Qualitative Evaluation

The qualitative evaluation involves gathering data on the unique qualitative characteristics of the community, identifying the externalities affecting the housing market, and identifying the key community leaders who can influence the community's reaction to a housing crisis.

Regulatory Constraints

Regulatory constraints are the rules, laws, and other ordinances created by a community that govern the development and use of housing. As noted earlier, regulatory constraints, including zoning and land-use restrictions and growth-management regulations, can have a significant influence on the cost and availability of housing. These regulatory constraints must be analyzed when evaluating a community's housing market for market failure.

The first step in analyzing regulatory constraints is to determine what constraints currently exist. This step entails developing a comprehensive list of existing regulations and what they allow and do not allow. For example, if growth-management regulations have been implemented, the analysis should identify the number and type and quality of housing units that can be developed each year. The review of land-use and zoning regulations should look for rulings on things such as minimum lot sizes; height restrictions; setback requirements; minimum or maximum square footage requirements; historic preservation; visual appeal; and who may live in a property, including rules about in-law apartments and cohabitation. The review should also examine the process and the actual time required to obtain the permits necessary to develop a piece of property. Finally, the review should note any incentives for affordable housing that exist in the current regulations.

Regulatory Constraints

Growth Management
  Limits on new development
  Limits on type of development permitted
  Delays in permitting and approvals
  Affordable housing incentives
  Impact fee requirements

Zoning and Land Use
  Lot size restrictions
  Height restrictions
  Setback requirements
  Minimum square footage requirements
  In-law apartment restrictions
  Cohabitation restrictions
  Impact fee requirements
  Visual appeal restrictions
  Historic preservation requirements

Once a comprehensive list has been created, the regulations should be evaluated to determine how they restrict the development of housing in the community and lead to higher housing costs. The key is to determine if these regulations are excessive. Historical data, pre- and post-regulation, should be examined to identify changes potentially resulting from regulation. Local developers and real estate professionals, community leaders, and government officials should be systematically interviewed to obtain their views about the results of the regulations.

The interview questions should focus on identifying what impact the regulations have had on the housing supply and costs. Do the growth-management regulations allow a sufficient number of units to be constructed each year to meet the needs of the population? If the number of households is growing faster than the number of new housing units allowed, supply and demand will become out of balance, resulting in rising housing prices. Have the lot size restrictions led to the development of more expensive housing units? Are there undersized lots in the community that are vacant but not buildable because they are too small under current zoning regulations? Are apartments permitted in single family houses? Is the use of these apartments limited to family members, such as in-laws or adult children, or can these units be rented to unrelated people? Can homeowners rent a bedroom in their homes to summer workers or local residents? Have rules about historic districts and historical preservation restricted housing development or renovation?

The interview questions can also be formulated to generate input on which regulations and restrictions might be removed or modified to increase the supply of market-rate and affordable housing. Developers and key community leaders are in the best position to know which regulations are working and which need modification in order to facilitate the creation of additional housing units.

For instance, the town of West Tisbury on Martha's Vineyard found that current zoning regulations made a number of vacant lots too small to be built on. But these lots were ideal locations on which to develop lower cost affordable housing. The simple solution, initially identified through the regulatory constraint review, allowed the lots to be developed as deed-restricted affordable housing.

Similar examples from other communities show that a limited modification of existing regulations can generate additional affordable housing units. The key is to identify the regulatory constraints, determine what impact these constraints have, and then probe the community leaders for potential solutions.

Topographic Constraints

Topographic constraints can also affect the supply of housing. This is particularly true in tourism communities that depend on their location and natural resources to attract tourists. Beaches and mountains are important parts of the tourism economy in many resort communities, and as a result the communities have imposed regulations that limit the development of these areas. Additionally, development of many areas, such as dunes, wetlands, flood plains, and coastal areas, have been restricted for environmental reasons. Overall development may be restricted when a community has limited capacity to provide additional fresh water and sanitation services. As a result, the available developable land is reduced, and housing and other development must take place in the nonrestricted areas. As the available land in the nonrestricted areas decreases, the cost of the land increases, and any housing constructed on this land becomes more expensive.

Topographic Constraints

Mountains
Beaches
Dunes and coastal areas
Wetlands
Flood plains
Fresh water limitations
Sanitation limitations

When evaluating a community for housing market failure, you must consider topographic constraints. The evaluation should identify the topographic constraints that affect the community, the reasons for these constraints, and the impact these constraints have on the supply of developable land in the community.

Topographic constraints can be identified through a physical review of the community; through a review of local scientific and geological maps and data, and local and regional regulations; and through interviews with local officials, such as those working in development and with the environment. If a community has significant topographic constraints and limited available land, one expected consequence is high housing costs. Topographic constraints are externalities that can lead to market failure.

Political Will

Because of their importance, political and governmental structure must be considered in evaluating a community; the willingness of key political leaders to implement any affordable housing interventions must also be evaluated.

The government structure should be outlined to show the form of government used at the local, regional, and state level; the government and government-sponsored agencies with responsibility for housing and housing development in the community; and the relative participation levels of community members in the local government through service on boards and committees. One outcome of this process may be the identification of multiple government or government-sponsored agencies with responsibility for the same tasks; for instance, agencies at the local and regional levels may have the same responsibilities, or there may be an absence of agencies with specific area responsibilities.

Once the government structure has been outlined, the key political players should be identified. The key players are those elected, appointed, or civil service officials in positions of power who can make or break a housing intervention. Examples include the mayor; members of the city council, county commission, or state legislature, particularly if they are outspoken about housing issues; the chairs of key legislative committees; and the appointed heads of the local housing authority and state housing finance agencies.

Key Political Leaders
Mayor
Members of the city council
County commissioners
State legislators
Chairs of key legislative committees
Head of the housing authority
Head of housing finance agencies
Head of planning and development

As my research shows, when a housing crisis occurs, sometimes a community will act to intervene in the housing market and sometimes it will not act. Political will makes the difference. The community must have the political will to act to address the housing market failure.

After the governmental structure has been outlined and the key players identified, the next step is to analyze the political will of a community through interviews with its leaders. The interview questions should emphasize the degree to which housing is a political issue in the community, the important issues and hot buttons of the political leaders regarding housing, and the leaders' willingness to tax or otherwise extract fees from the community for housing. Do the leaders believe that market failure has occurred or is likely to occur? Are they willing to tax the locals for housing? Are they willing or able to tax tourists for housing? Are they willing to risk political capital to deal with housing issues? Does the political structure recognize a community crisis? Does the political will exist to address a housing crisis?

Community Will

The community's informal leadership and social structure must also be evaluated to determine willingness to intervene in the housing market to correct market failure. Informal leaders include religious and business leaders, community activists, the community elite, and others with real or perceived positions of power and influence in the community. Although they do not hold elective or appointive positions, these informal leaders can exert significant influence on community members and political leaders.

Key Informal Community Leaders
Religious leaders
Business leaders
Community activists
Community elites
Others active in community housing efforts

The first step in evaluating a community's social structure is to identify these leaders, their roles in the community, and the constituencies they represent. Often they can be identified during interviews with political and governmental leaders. They also can be identified through their mention in articles about housing in the local newspapers and other community publications.

Like political will, community will is needed to implement an effective housing intervention. The community must be willing to join with the political leaders to effect the implementation of interventions. If community resistance is strong or the community at large disagrees with the political leaders, an intervention is less likely to be successful.

The informal social leaders should be interviewed to obtain data on the roles they play in the community, how they achieved those roles, the constituencies they represent, and whether they agree or disagree with the political leaders on housing issues.

Other questions should focus on the community's social structure, whether it has a real or perceived class system, its willingness to welcome newcomers, the degree to which newcomers integrate into the community, and—in tourism communities—the degree to which second-home owners actively participate in the community.

The informal leaders should also be asked their opinions on housing. Is the community experiencing a housing crisis? Is housing an important issue in the community? Is the core of the community being eroded by unaffordable housing? Is the community willing to tax itself to pay for affordable housing?

The data gathered from the informal leaders should be evaluated to determine if they recognize a community crisis, and if they believe the community is willing and able to intervene in the market and address housing issues. Does the community will exist?

For an intervention strategy to be successfully developed and implemented in a community, the political leaders and informal leaders must recognize a housing crisis, and both political will and community will to act must be present. Without that recognition and willingness to act, it is unlikely that intervention strategies will be pursued.

Housing Market Evaluation

Once the indicators, macro and micro trends, leadership, and housing market externalities have been reviewed, an overall evaluation of the housing market can be performed. This evaluation should include an assessment of current and prospective market failure conditions in the housing market, an assessment of the community's strengths and weaknesses, and an identification of the issues affecting the local housing market.

As stated earlier, market failure can occur when significant external factors—externalities such as regulatory and topographic constraints and second-home demand by buyers from external economies—restrict the free functioning of the market. The evaluation of the community's housing market for market failure must include the identification and evaluation of these externalities. The data gathered during the indicator and qualitative evaluations are combined and evaluated during the housing market evaluation.

The housing market evaluation is best presented with an example. Consider the study of Whistler (presented in chapter 9). The indicator evaluation identifies (1) tourism as the most important part of the community's economy, (2) significant second-home demand, and (3) free-market housing that was unaffordable to typical residents. The qualitative evaluation identifies (1) an absolute cap on future development, which was expected to be reached by 2004; (2) significant topographical constraints, resulting from the surrounding mountains and wetlands; and (3) limitations on available natural resources, all of which acted to limit housing development in the community. Finally, the macro trend analysis identifies two factors driving the demand for second homes: a favorable Canadian currency exchange rate with the United States and the attractiveness of real estate as an investment; and the micro trend analysis identifies an aging population because fewer young families could afford to purchase housing and move into the community.

Combining these individual factors, we see that significant externalities are affecting the housing market, resulting in its failure to function efficiently. We also see a community experiencing a housing crisis, which, based on the trend analysis and theory of market failure, can be expected to worsen over time.

Evaluation of the Whistler data pinpoints some important strengths in the community: notably an awareness of housing issues by the political and informal leaders of the community, and their willingness to intervene in the housing market. The evaluation also notes some significant weaknesses, including a growth cap that restricts all future development and a depleted fund for affordable housing development. These strengths and weaknesses will affect future affordable housing interventions by the community. The strengths can be leveraged. The weaknesses will have to be overcome.

Finally, the evaluation identifies significant issues affecting Whistler—the continued growth of second homes, an aging population, and a continued demand for workers by the successful tourism industry—issues that indicate a continuing housing crisis and that will have to be addressed if housing market intervention strategies are to be successfully implemented.

3

Community Intervention

Once an evaluation has identified housing market failure conditions and the existence of a current or prospective housing crisis, it is time to engage in the second phase of the Community Evaluation and Intervention Process in order to correct the market failure.

The intervention process contains seven steps: the community creates a housing vision, defines housing goals, analyzes existing resources and resource gaps, identifies necessary actions, pinpoints critical success factors, devises an intervention plan, and implements a series of interventions. (See chart next page)

Creating a Housing Vision

One of the most important steps in the housing intervention process is the creation of a housing vision for the community. When a community formulates a housing vision, it defines the way it wants its housing to look in the future. If the community could wave a magic wand and see the future, what housing would be available for its residents and local workers?

A housing vision should be stated simply. For instance, "In five years, 50 percent of the workers employed in local businesses will live in the community," or "Housing will be available in our community at affordable levels for all those who work here, from the lowest paid to the highest paid."

Community Evaluation and Intervention Process

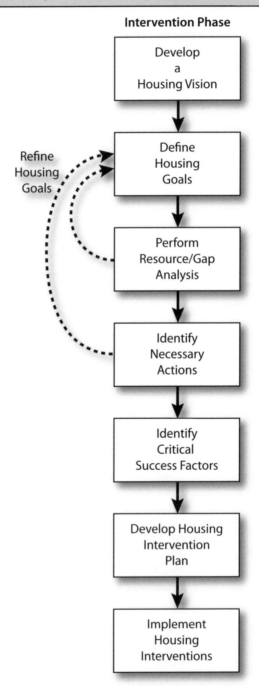

Intervention Phase

But the visioning process is complex, and care must be taken to assure that it is facilitated effectively and is inclusive. It should involve participation by representatives from all sectors of the community, including political leaders, informal leaders, appointed and elected civic officials, local businesses, the local real estate and construction industries, current and prospective residents of the community's affordable housing, and any other interested community members. The more inclusive the process, the more likely the participants will buy into the results. If the key community members are present as the housing vision is created, and their input has been heard and incorporated, the less likely they are to resist implementation of the vision.

Typically, the visioning process entails holding one or more community meetings at which the key representatives and other interested parties formulate the vision. The meetings might be held on a Saturday, over several weeknights, or whenever is most convenient for the most people. Ideally the meetings should be held away from people's normal places of business so those attending can focus fully on the process and not be distracted by routine workday interruptions. The meetings are best held in a facility where the participants can sit in a circle facing each other, so all have equal status, rather than classroom style, which may give those at the front table a higher perceived status. Community rooms and school cafeterias make ideal meeting places because there is space for the tables and chairs to be placed in a circle. Offices and auditoriums are less than ideal because those sitting at the desk or on stage have more control over the meeting and a higher perceived status than those in the audience.

An experienced, outside, professional facilitator is a must for a community creating a housing vision. He or she is hired simply to facilitate the process, has no vested interest in the community or the vision developed, and hence can best hear the arguments presented by all participants. Using local facilitators or paid community staff, no matter how experienced they may be, is a bad idea. They may be influenced by their own agenda, or may defer to their superiors or to those with positions of power in the community. An outside facilitator is not personally involved and is less likely to be influenced by the existing community political and social structure.

Whistler is an example of a community that continually re-creates and updates its visions. It has revised its housing vision every few years for the last decade. The sustainability of the local environment and of the resort as a tourist destination are important issues in Whistler, and the community has used the visioning process to handle them effectively. The town's latest housing vision projects more than fifteen years into the future.

Defining Housing Goals

A community's housing vision is a broad-reaching look at the future. To achieve the vision, the community must intervene in the housing market and develop or facilitate the development of housing units. The next step in the intervention process, more finite and concrete than creating a vision, is defining measurable and achievable housing goals. To define the goals, the community must consider its vision and the issues identified in its market evaluation.

Housing goals can be established using the same facilitated community meeting process used to create the housing vision. Input of different opinions from the community is critical. To achieve the goals, the support of political leaders, informal leaders, and community members will be necessary. This support will be easier to obtain when the players participate in the goal-setting process.

Housing goals define what the community wants to achieve (a measurable factor) and by when (a time frame). For example: Build X affordable units over the next three years; provide housing for an additional Y families who work in the community in the following year. Martha's Vineyard set a five-year goal of creating 205 new and permanently affordable housing units. That is a measurable goal with a finite time frame. In five years, and at checkpoints along the way, Martha's Vineyard can compare its goal to the number of housing units created and measure the relative success or failure of its affordable housing efforts. Looking fifteen years into the future, Whistler sees an aging population and the need for Olympic housing, and has begun the process of developing housing goals for the next several decades.

The process of defining goals should deliberately and immediately follow the visioning process and precede the resource/gap analysis. The initial goals established reflect what needs to be done to achieve the vision and therefore should not be constrained by resource shortages. If initial goals were established after the resource/gap analysis, they would likely include some downward adjustment resulting from available resource constraints and therefore might not show what is necessary to achieve the vision. The housing goals should reflect what is necessary; and resource constraints can be addressed through necessary actions and implementation plans. The initial housing goals can always be refined later if it becomes impossible to find the resources needed to carry them out.

Analyzing Resources and Resource Gaps

After defining its housing goals, the community should conduct a resource and gap analysis. What resources are needed to achieve the goals? What resources exist in the community and at the regional, state, and national levels that the community can use? Where are the gaps in the existing resources?

Resources necessary for an effective housing market intervention include money; the programs and methods to provide the housing; qualified personnel to develop, implement, and monitor the programs; and support from the community and its political and informal leaders.

Necessary Housing Resources

Money

Means and methods to provide housing:
    Programs
    Organizations
    Legislative support

Qualified personnel for:
    Housing development
    Program implementation and management
    Program monitoring

Community support from:
    Political leaders
    Informal leaders
    Community members

Let's start with money. Monetary resources for affordable housing can come from within the community or from outside. Traditional sources of money for affordable housing include state and national housing finance agencies that provide grants and loans for housing development, and national equity programs such as the low-income-housing tax credit program in the United States. Nontraditional sources of money include the local community itself. Each of the successful tourism communities I studied used local funds as a primary source of capital for affordable housing development. Aspen imposed a real estate transfer tax, and Whistler imposed an impact fee on real estate developers; the proceeds go to a housing development fund in each town. Martha's Vineyard is leveraging the wealth of the island's summer residents to raise funds for rental assistance and program administration.

The analysis of resources available to achieve the defined housing goals must consider money available from both traditional and nontraditional sources, from outside the community and from within. Be creative. The more monetary resources that can be identified, the easier it will be to achieve housing goals. Lack of monetary resources is a gap, and will need to be dealt with.

In addition to money, a community needs the means and methods to facilitate the development of housing, and it needs qualified people to work with the housing programs. The resource analysis should identify the local entities and people with explicit responsibility for housing, such as the housing authority or nonprofit housing developers, and it should also identify those whose experience, expertise, and relationships can be leveraged to help provide housing. The latter group might include local developers, real estate professionals, and concerned community members. Any lack of development methods or qualified people is a gap to be addressed.

Finally, the implementation of an effective housing intervention depends greatly on support from the community and from its political and informal leaders. Do they have the will to act? The community and its political and informal leaders can be a resource if they believe a housing crisis exists and they are willing to expend political and social capital to address the issues. But if these groups have not bought into the existence of a community crisis or if they are not willing to expend the necessary political and social capital, then a gap exists.

Identifying Necessary Actions

A housing vision has been developed, housing goals established, and existing resources and gaps identified. Now it is time to note the actions necessary to move toward the goals. What steps need to be taken to address each gap and turn it into a resource? What actions will access the community's resources and leverage its strengths?

Again, an example can be drawn from my research. Martha's Vineyard identified two significant resources on the island: a large number of wealthy people who summered there and generally cared about the place, and a history of charitable giving from those summer residents. They also identified a gap: a lack of money for affordable housing programs and for the support of the agencies charged with providing affordable housing. Once the resources and gaps were laid side by side, the necessary actions became obvious: leverage the history of charitable giving, and develop a program to solicit from wealthy summer residents charitable donations to be used to support affordable housing programs and the operation of affordable housing agencies.

Pinpointing Critical Success Factors

Once necessary actions have been identified, critical success factors—those that can make or break the intervention—should be determined. Which steps and events must go right for the intervention to be a success? Which will cause the intervention to fail if they go wrong?

For example, the ability of Martha's Vineyard to access its wealthy summer residents and receive donations from them was a critical success factor. If its actions were successful, funding for affordable housing would be available; but if the prospective donors either could not be accessed or did not donate, then the funding would not be available and the community would not be able to implement the affordable housing programs.

Chapter 5 discusses the critical factors for successful housing interventions that my research has singled out.

Devising a Housing Intervention Plan

To devise the housing intervention plan, compile the results of the preceding steps—the vision, goals, resources and gaps, and the actions necessary to access the resources or address the gaps—into one formulation.

The housing intervention plan should describe in detail how the interventions proposed by the community will be implemented. The plan should describe the interventions themselves; the time frame for their implementation; their goals; the measurements to be used to assess their effectiveness; the sources of funds to be used; the actions necessary to access these sources; the organizations, agencies, and other entities that will be involved in implementing the interventions; the qualifications of the personnel involved; the political, social, and community leaders from whom buy-in will be needed; and the current degree of buy-in from these leaders. Finally, the housing intervention plan should describe arrangements for an ongoing monitoring and evaluation of the housing market.

**Elements of the Housing
Intervention Plan**

Housing vision
Housing goals
Interventions to be implemented
Time frame
Measures of effectiveness or success
Sources of funds
Key personnel and organizations
Specified organizational responsibilities
Actions needed
Critical success factors
Plan for implementation
Plan for ongoing monitoring

Martha's Vineyard provides a good example of how a housing intervention plan was compiled from the individual components. As mentioned earlier, Martha's Vineyard established an overall goal of creating 205 new affordable housing units over the next five years. To meet this goal, the community needs to implement several programs, each with its own resource/gap analysis, necessary actions, and critical success factors. The community's intervention plan includes the aforementioned accessing of local wealth for funding, actions to change local zoning regulations to allow development of affordable housing on undersized lots, and actions to develop a program to move older housing units that would otherwise be torn down to interior locations on the island for use as affordable housing. The individual programs, each with its own goals, are combined in the overall intervention plan, which is focused on meeting the overall goal.

Implementing Housing Interventions

Once the housing intervention plan has been devised, buy-in has been received from the community, resources have been tapped, and gaps addressed, it is time to act.

During implementation, expected results and time frames should be constantly monitored so that mid-course corrections can be incorporated as needed. Changes can also be made during implementation to keep the plan on track, moving toward the goal and vision.

4

Community Monitoring

One of the more interesting findings of my research was that interventions can correct for market failure in the short term, but the market may fail again over time. What happened in Aspen vividly illustrates this point. Many people consider Aspen to be one of the most successful examples of a community that has intervened in the housing market to provide affordable housing for its residents. Aspen's interventions began about thirty years ago, and currently 64 percent of the residents live in affordable housing, a higher percentage than can be found in most, if not all, other tourism communities worldwide. By almost any measure, Aspen's housing interventions have been successful.

But all is not well with Aspen. As my research shows, community leaders are concerned about the continued effectiveness of their affordable housing programs. The number of second homes in Aspen continues to grow, and each time a primary residence is converted to a second home, market rate housing used by local residents is removed from the system. Additionally, the existing residents of Aspen's affordable housing units are beginning to approach retirement age. As they retire, many continue to occupy their affordable housing units. Thus those units are not available for the workers who replace the retirees, and additional affordable units are needed. The housing market in Aspen continues to fail.

As seen in Aspen and other communities, the effectiveness of housing market interventions is not static. That is, an intervention program that is effective today may fail tomorrow because conditions change with time, and new factors may be introduced that diminish the program's effectiveness.

There is therefore a need for monitoring, which is the final phase of the Community Evaluation and Intervention Process. Communities must continually evaluate the housing market for market failure, look for the appearance of new or changed externalities, check the continued availability of resources needed for the existing interventions, and assess the effectiveness of those interventions.

New Externalities

Externalities are a condition of market failure. If a community's interventions are successful, the effects of the externalities on the housing market are mitigated. But if new externalities develop, market failure conditions may re-appear. The housing market needs to be continually monitored and evaluated for the existence of new or developing externalities.

For example, although Aspen has created a significant number of affordable housing units for residents employed in the local workforce, some of them continue to live in market rate units. Aspen is relying on the market for part of its housing stock and did not anticipate growth in the number of second homes. As more market rate units—sold by workers who want to retire and cash in on their housing investments—are turned into second homes (the second-home externality), new local workers are unable to find or afford housing.

A new, expanded second-home externality has developed, resulting in housing market failure and a growing community crisis. By continually monitoring and evaluating the housing market, a community can become aware of new externalities as they develop, and can respond with an intervention before the problem becomes a crisis.

Changes in Local Resources

As described more fully in chapter 3, the effective use of local resources is often key to the design and implementation of an effective housing market intervention. Like externalities, local resources are not static and may change over time. Therefore, communities should continually monitor the local resources relied on for housing interventions, and should continually identify and evaluate potential local resources.

Community Evaluation and Intervention Process

Monitoring Phase

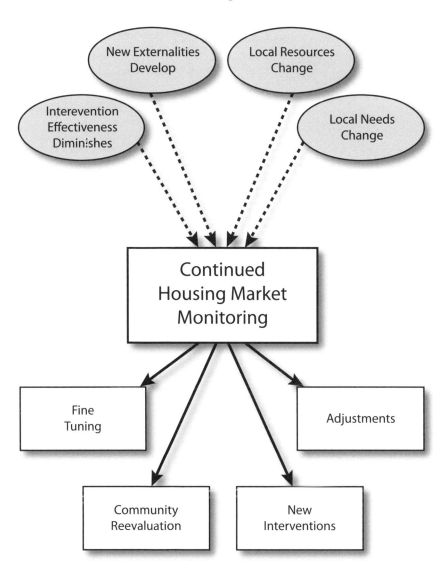

Whistler has relied on an impact fee paid by local developers as a source of funds to run its housing programs and as equity capital for affordable housing developed by the community. But Whistler is effectively built-out under the current growth cap, meaning that no more development can take place. Hence, no more impact fees will be paid to the local housing fund, and the local housing authority will have to seek other means of funding its operations. A local resource that had been relied on is no longer available.

In contrast, Provincetown is attempting to create a new local resource by seeking approval from the state legislature for the imposition of a real estate property transfer tax, the proceeds of which will be paid into a fund for affordable housing development. Should the legislature allow the imposition of this tax, the local resources available to Provincetown, and to all other communities in the state, will change. If Martha's Vineyard and other tourism communities in Massachusetts are monitoring their housing intervention programs, they will be able to identify and use this additional local resource.

Changes in Other Resources

Housing resources available to a community at the regional, state, and national level can also be expected to change over time and should be monitored by the community.

For example, consider the changes that took place in federal and state programs for affordable housing finance in the late 1980s and early 1990s. Before the late 1980s, many of those programs offered money for affordable housing development in the form of grants given directly to developers and communities. Many of these programs had ceased by the early 1990s, and were replaced by equity investment programs such as the low-income housing tax credit program. A community relying on the former programs for their housing interventions would have to learn to use the new programs.

Changes in Local Needs

Housing intervention programs should be monitored for changes in local needs. A housing market evaluation performed many years ago, or even a few years ago, may be out of date. The characteristics and needs of the community may have changed, and the housing interventions may need to change as well. Communities with successful housing market interventions should continually monitor their interventions for effectiveness.

Monitoring can identify shifts in the local economy, shifts in demographics, and shifts in the needs of residents. The interventions needed in a mature tourism community with an aging population and an increasing number of retirees or prospective retires occupying the community's affordable housing are different from the interventions needed in a growing tourism community. In one case the need may be for more smaller units for seniors; in the other case the need may be for family units. As a tourism community matures, the housing needs change, and the interventions must change as well. The characteristics and needs of a community must be continually monitored, and the housing intervention programs must be modified in response to changing needs.

Diminished Intervention Effectiveness

The effectiveness of existing interventions should be monitored. As discussed earlier, the goals of housing intervention programs must be defined and measurable. Monitoring the effectiveness of interventions can be accomplished through a periodic comparison of program results with program goals. Are the interventions working as planned? Are they serving the community as planned? Do they need some fine tuning or major adjustments?

With its long history of successful housing intervention, Aspen has some program features that provide insight into how intervention effectiveness diminishes over time. Aspen uses deed restrictions to control many of the affordable housing units developed in the community. During the initial housing interventions, some deed restrictions were set to expire after a certain period such as twenty or thirty years, after which the units would revert to market rate housing. As these deed restrictions expire, the effectiveness of the original interventions diminishes. Recognizing this gap, Aspen has adjusted its programs so that deed restrictions now extend for ninety-nine years or more.

Summary

The Community Evaluation and Intervention Process is a proven methodology for evaluating a community's housing market and for creating and implementing housing intervention strategies to repair housing market failure.

In the first phase of the Community Evaluation and Intervention Process, the quantitative and qualitative indicators of the health of a community's housing market are collected, analyzed, and assessed; and the externalities that affect the free functioning of the housing market and can lead to market failure are evaluated. In the second phase, the steps a community must pursue to create an effective housing market intervention are described and implemented. In the third phase, key areas are identified and continually monitored to assure the ongoing effectiveness of interventions.

5

Lessons For The Housing Practitioner

As mentioned in chapter 3, certain factors are critical to the success of housing market interventions. My research has identified those factors and points to policy implications for housing practitioners who will use the Community Evaluation and Intervention Process to determine if the housing market in their community is experiencing market failure and to create, implement, and monitor housing interventions.

Critical Success Factors

Critical success factors are those that must be present and must go right if a project is to succeed. The eight factors required for successful housing market interventions are:

1. Political will
2. Community will
3. Housing vision
4. Housing plan
5. Political and community buy-in
6. Funding
7. Land
8. Organizational capacity

Political and Community Will

A community must want to deal with affordable housing issues and must have the will to develop and implement solutions. When confronted with a housing market failure and community crisis, the community must be willing to intervene. Aspen, Martha's Vineyard, and Whistler achieved positive results because they possessed the political and community will to address their affordable housing issues. They saw the lack of affordable housing for their residents as a serious issue that affected the core of the community, and they took action to implement a solution. Their leaders, whether elected, appointed, or unofficial, were willing to expend political capital to get the issues on the table and to formulate plans to handle the issues; and community members were willing to fund affordable housing programs. In contrast, Provincetown did not possess the will to react when faced with the community crisis of a housing market failure, and hence did not intervene; it did not achieve a positive result.

Vision and Plan

Successful models for affordable housing may differ from one community to the next in their details, but they will all contain three major components: a vision, a plan or strategy to achieve the vision, and the development of programs to implement the vision. The leaders in Aspen, Whistler, and Martha's Vineyard recognized the need for affordable housing for their residents and articulated a vision for their communities. Using this vision as a guide, they formulated a plan for including affordable housing in the community and created programs that facilitated the development of affordable housing for community residents. Aspen's housing vision was created by its early community leaders. Whistler's housing vision was created as part of the overall development strategy for the resort, and includes significant elements borrowed from the experience of other tourism communities, including Aspen. In each of the successful communities, the vision and plan were developed with input from community leaders and community residents. Each community has a written housing plan and treats it like a living document, constantly modifying and revising it as housing and conditions in the community change.

Buy-In

Buy-in from political leaders, informal community leaders, and the community itself is necessary for a housing intervention to be effective.

Buy-in can be achieved by including leaders and community members in the discussion of the issues and in the development of the solutions; by developing solutions that fit the type and character of the community; and by demonstrating the effectiveness of the intervention models through example, either in the subject community or in a similar community. The key is to provide reasons to accept rather than reject affordable housing.

In Aspen, Whistler, and Martha's Vineyard, support from local leaders was used (1) to change local regulation in order to enable the development of affordable housing, (2) for the direct development of housing, and (3) to establish funding programs that relied on taxes and impact fees. The successful communities actively cultivated and maintained political support for affordable housing. In both Aspen and Whistler, affordable housing is a political issue, and candidates for office must articulate their position on affordable housing during the election process.

In contrast, Provincetown did not achieve community and political buy-in, and it was not successful in providing affordable housing. The housing issues were addressed in an exclusionary, top-down process rather than through inclusion. Those community members who were interested in affordable housing but were excluded from the process felt unhappy and powerless to change the situation. Provincetown presents a lesson: affordable housing efforts that exclude certain leaders or segments of the community and that do not win broad buy-in from community members and political leaders will be difficult to implement and may not be effective.

Funding

Programs for funding, another critical success factor in the achievement of affordable housing, should be established during the planning stage in communities developed explicitly for tourism; otherwise, funding should be established as tourism begins to become important in the local economy. The resource and gap analysis must include the study of funding. A community's housing intervention plan should identify the funding needs for affordable housing and the sources of funds to meet these needs.

Funding programs should be designed such that affordable housing costs are borne primarily by tourists and second-home owners, and not by local residents. Aspen, Whistler, and Martha's Vineyard used a combination of impact fees, real estate transfer taxes, sales taxes, and private donations as funding sources. Because these sources are flexible, locally controlled, and not subject to limiting federal and state restrictions on income, they can be used to address the unique housing issues in each community.

Land

Land for the development of affordable housing units is another critical success factor. Because land will be more expensive during the later stages of the tourism lifecycle, a land bank should be established before tourism develops, if possible. When specifically developing a tourism community, land should be designated for affordable resident housing in the planning stage; a strategy should be devised to purchase or reserve the land before other development occurs on the site or land prices rise. Incentives should be offered to commercial and residential real estate developers to set aside land for affordable housing within their developments. Absence of a sufficient land bank will make public development of affordable housing more difficult and more costly because land may have to be purchased at free-market prices.

Organizational Capacity

Finally, the community needs an organizational infrastructure, qualified people, and well-conceived programs to successfully develop affordable housing. Aspen, Whistler, and Martha's Vineyard achieved positive results partly because they had organizations specifically devoted to providing affordable housing for community residents and to administering the existing affordable housing programs. These organizations were staffed by full-time, experienced, professional people. A working relationship existed between the housing organizations and the town planning and development organizations. In contrast, Provincetown, which did not achieve positive results, had a housing authority that was staffed by just one part-time employee and was open for only a limited number of hours each week; and no town staff members had specific responsibility for housing.

Policy Implications

Policy makers, planners, housing professionals, and other community and political leaders in tourism communities should recognize that the market will not supply the needed housing when externalities are present in the housing market. The community must intervene to assist in providing affordable resident housing. The externalities influencing housing supply (growth-management and land-use and zoning regulations, and topographical constraints) are such that market housing development will emphasize high-end, expensive housing to the exclusion of affordable housing; and second-home demand will remove existing resident housing from the system, leading to unaffordable housing and a community crisis.

Whenever possible, tourism communities should be proactive in their housing market intervention, planning for and developing affordable housing units before a crisis occurs. When communities plan new tourism development, they should include affordable housing for community residents in their plans. Aspen and Whistler, the two most successful communities I studied, were proactive in addressing housing issues, acting before a market failure had occurred.

Policy Implications
1.   Recognize the conditions of market failure.
2.   Be proactive.
3.   Monitor housing affordability.
4.   Monitor second-home growth.
5.   Remain focused on interventions over market cycles.
6.   Leverage local resources for funding.
7.   Use a mix of public and private development.
8.   Provide a mix of ownership and rental units.
9.   Learn from other communities.
10.   Examine each community as a unique entity.
11.   Recognize that interventions are not static and require constant modification and renewal as market conditions change.

Second-home demand is an important externality that drives housing prices in tourism communities. The conversion of existing free-market housing units to second homes has the effect of removing from the
system housing units that had been available for workers and community residents, leading to increased prices and displaced residents. Tourism communities should monitor changes in the number and percentage of second homes in the community to identify any trends that indicate a reduction in resident housing units; and they should monitor the
ratio of housing prices to income in order to identify changes in relative
housing affordability. When the community becomes aware of negative
trends affecting housing, it can intervene proactively before market failure occurs.

Existing tourism communities should also establish a source of funds
for affordable housing, offer incentives for private development of affordable housing, and create an affordable housing infrastructure. The community's housing market interventions should be ongoing, encompassing
both strong and weak economic periods. A housing crisis most likely will
be reached at the peak of an economic and housing cycle, when housing prices are the highest. At the peak of the market, intervention costs
will also be greatest. By continually intervening in the housing market,
a community can take advantage of lower costs during non-peak periods and will have developed additional affordable units before the next
market peak and housing crisis.

The community should look to local resources for funding. Aspen,
Whistler, and Martha's Vineyard developed affordable housing funding
programs that leveraged local resources, allowing the flexibility to develop affordable housing in keeping with the character of their community,
and allowing eligibility criteria that recognize the unique combination
of high housing costs and low wages in tourism communities. Using local resources for funding frees a community from the restrictions found
in federal and state housing programs.

A mix of affordable housing programs should be applied, including
programs for the public development of housing that use the land bank
and public housing funds, and programs that provide incentives for
private developers and community residents to create affordable housing units. Incentives should be focused on including affordable housing

in new commercial and residential development, on infill development, and on the creation of apartments, suites, and rooms in existing housing. The affordable housing should be sized and styled to fit the character of the community.

The housing programs should supply a mix of housing units in multiple sizes, from single rooms and studio apartments up to multiple-bedroom family units. A mix of ownership and rental units should be offered to allow lifestyle flexibility and to assist in obtaining resident ownership of the community.

A community should learn from other places and from other programs as it develops its affordable housing programs. Whistler studied Aspen and other winter recreation communities as it developed its housing programs. Martha's Vineyard combined a history of charitable giving from the island's wealthy long-term residents with a funding model previously used for land conservation on the island, and created a source of funds to revitalize its affordable housing fund.

Each of the four communities of Aspen, Whistler, Martha's Vineyard, and Provincetown is unique; my research did not identify among them a standard threshold of second homes or housing affordability beyond which intervention is required. From a policy perspective, it is necessary to monitor and examine each community individually for market failure and to develop programs that reflect the uniqueness of the community.

The final housing policy implication for tourism communities is that because conditions change over time, success in solving housing market failures is relative. Affordable housing programs must be renewed or modified repeatedly. Aspen and Whistler have been successful in providing affordable housing for a significant number of community residents, yet the demand for second homes and the continued conversion of existing residential units to second homes is straining the communities; affordable housing units have not replaced all the units lost to second homes. Although these communities have made significant strides, they continually face new problems as housing demands change and the community evolves. Communities are not static; new externalities appear, adversely affecting the housing market; and as a result, housing interventions must constantly evolve to keep pace with the changes.

Part 2
Theoretical Foundations

6

Housing Market Economics

This chapter presents a brief overview of classical economic theory and the theory of market failure. The key premise underlying the housing market research conducted and the housing intervention processes discussed is that the housing market in the communities studied has failed as the result of externalities, and that the community must intervene if it is to correct the market failure and provide housing for its members.

The Theory of Market Failure

A constant argument among economists regards the efficiency of markets. The basic theories of classical economics state that over time the supply and demand for a good or service will continually be adjusted so that supply equals demand. In contrast, the market failure branch of economic theory argues that this equality of supply and demand can occur only when the market is free of constraints, and that when constraints do exist, the market may fail to function freely.

The Classical Argument

Adam Smith introduced the concept of the "invisible hand" of the market to classical economics, whereby a perfectly functioning market mechanism acts to adjust supply and demand and keep market conditions in balance. In this market, government intervention is thought to be unnecessary and unwelcome (Smith 1776 a and b). In *The Wealth of Nations,* Smith writes:

> *No regulation of commerce can increase the
> quantity of industry in any society beyond what
> its capital can maintain. It can only divert a
> part of it into a direction into which it might
> not otherwise have gone; and it is by no means
> certain that this artificial direction is likely to
> be more advantageous to the society than that
> into which it would have gone of its own ac-
> cord. (1776 b, 30)*

From this base, classical economists argue that when the market is free of constraints, it will constantly adjust so that the supply of a good or service will equal the demand for the same good or service. That is, the market will be in equilibrium. The market will adjust for temporary disequilibriums through changes in the supply and demand.

Conditions of the classical economic model include perfect information, minimal or no transaction costs, and a market free of constraints, in which labor and capital are free to move to their most productive uses. In classical economic theory, efficient markets lead to an efficient output mix and to what is known as Pareto optimal distribution of goods or services. Pareto optimality occurs at the maximum production point, where you cannot make one producer or consumer better off without making another one worse off.

The key premise of the classical economist's argument is that the market be free of constraints. When constraints are imposed, the market's efficient functioning begins to falter.

The Case for Market Failure

For more than a decade, economists have debated extensively about the efficiency of the market versus its failure. Does Adam Smith's "invisible hand" continually act to bring the market into equilibrium, or are there other factors that interfere with this invisible hand and cause the market to fail to achieve Pareto optimality?

The market failure economist argues that these other factors, known as externalities, do in fact exist in the form of market imperfections and constraints that interfere with and weaken the functioning of the market, and cause the market to become inefficient and fail. These constraints and imperfections cause the market to fail to achieve Pareto optimality. It is not the invisible hand posited by Adam Smith that will correct the market but an intervention by the state (that is, the government or the community).

By the early twentieth century, the economics literature began to contain significant works questioning Smith's theory and introducing the premises on which market failure theory is based. Market failure as a branch of economics began in the 1930s and continues to this day, having been embraced by such famous and Nobel Prize–winning economists as Arthur Pigou (1932), John Maynard Keynes (1936), Paul Samuelson (1954), and Francis Bator (1958).

Pigou, in his seminal work *The Economics of Welfare*, introduced the external cost concepts built upon by Samuelson and Bator in their theories of market failure. Pigou cites the potential for a divergence between the goals of private investment and social goals:

> *In general, industrialists are interested, not in the social, but only in the private, net product of their operations. . . . It will not tend to bring about the equality in the values of the marginal social net products except when marginal private net product and marginal social net product are identical. (172)*

Pigou cites a divergence between private net product and social net product that occurs when it is difficult if not impossible to obtain payment from parties who have received incidental benefits from an action, or to make payment to those who have been burdened with a cost. According to Pigou, the market does not correct these divergences, and intervention is necessary:

> *When there is a divergence between these two sorts of marginal net products, self-interest will not, therefore, tend to make the national dividend a maximum; and, consequently, certain specific acts of interference with normal economic processes may be expected, not to diminish, but to increase the dividend. (172)*

In addition, Pigou took issue with the assumptions of classical economics, arguing that the market did not always achieve equilibrium on its own, and that enlightened government intervention could be preferable to unregulated laissez-faire policies.

In 1954, in "The Pure Theory of Public Expenditure," Paul Samuelson introduced the concept of market failure to modern economic theory. Samuelson starts with a model of a Pareto optimal economy—in which no one can be made better off without making someone else worse off, in which there is perfect knowledge and perfect competition, and in which all factors receive their appropriate marginal productivities—and introduces the concept of public expenditure and its theoretical impact on Pareto optimality. Public expenditure acts to maintain the competitive pricing of private goods by restricting the ability of any one selfish person to "snatch" the benefit of the goods. Public expenditure is necessary to maintain Pareto optimality by restricting the ability of persons to receive a benefit they did not pay for at the expense of the owner of that benefit (Samuelson 1954). The public expenditure cited by Samuelson, necessary because of the divergence between the private and social net product and the impossibility of assigning costs and collecting payments, is the same as the divergence cited by Pigou.

Samuelson and others use the concepts of welfare economics in creating these theories. Welfare economics refers to the efforts of an individual or society to achieve optimal allocation of resources to the benefit of all. That is, to achieve Pareto optimality.

In 1958, Francis Bator wrote one of the defining works of market failure theory, *The Anatomy of Market Failure*. Bator argues that the central premise of welfare economics, the duality theorem, fails, leading to inefficient markets and a failure to achieve Pareto optimality. Bator identifies five types of failure that can occur. The first is failure of existence. Pareto efficient production and exchange assumes the existence of a complete set of marginal-rate-of-substitution equalities. Goods may be freely substituted. When marginal-rate-of-substitution equalities do not occur, a failure of existence condition results. The second type, failure by signal, occurs when the configuration of inputs and outputs, evaluated in terms of price parameters, fails to yield a maximum profit position for each producer (i.e., a different configuration of prices for inputs and outputs is needed for profit maximization). The third type, failure by incentive, will occur when the configuration of inputs and outputs yields non-negative profits for all producers. Since profits are non-negative, production occurs, but profits are not maximized (Bator 1958).

Pareto optimality requires perfect competition and a fully functioning market mechanism in all markets. Bator argues that this requires many producers in every market; if there are fewer producers, the input, output, and price mechanisms will become distorted, and Pareto optimality will not be achieved. The fourth type of failure, failure by structure, will result (Bator 1958).

Bator's final type of failure is by enforcement. Failure by enforcement results from "arbitrary legal and organizational 'imperfections,' or feasibility limitation on 'keeping book,' such as leave some inputs and outputs 'hidden,' or preclude their explicit allocation or capture by market processes" (1958, 39).

Having identified the types of failure, Bator next identifies the causes of market failure. He broadly defines the cause as "externalities" (1958, 47). Externalities are costs or benefits that are external to the market price mechanism. They lead to a faulty price mechanism, which in turn leads to an allocation of inputs and outputs that are not optimal in terms of price, profit, and performance. Since the inputs and outputs are not allocated optimally, Pareto efficiency is not achieved.

As discussed throughout this book, externalities exist in tourism community housing markets in three forms: government-imposed regulations, second-home buyers from external economies, and topographical constraints.

Market Failure and Housing

Economists view the housing market through one of three primary theories: classical laissez-faire market theory, social development theory, and market failure theory.

Classical laissez-faire economic theorists would argue that housing is but one use of an individual's resources and that people are free to consume as much or as little housing as they chose. Classical economic theorists would also argue that the invisible hand of the market would act to adjust for disequilibirums in housing supply and demand and that the market will achieve Pareto optimality. As my research shows, significant externalities in the housing markets in tourism communities cause Pareto optimality not to be achieved.

Both social development and market failure theory argue for the intervention of the state in the housing market. Their motivations, however, are different. Market failure theorists argue that the market intervention is necessary to correct the inefficiencies and failures in the market caused by ownership, technical, and public-good externalities.

Social development theorists argue for intervention in the housing market for the betterment of community and society. Their primary argument is that adequate housing yields social as well as economic benefits. The social benefits include decreased social deviance, political and social stability, increased health, and increased education. Intervening in the housing market will assist in creating these benefits. The interventions are necessary for the benefit of society overall. Social development theorists also argue that inadequate housing results from income inequality and that housing subsidies should be used as a means of correcting this inequality.

Market failure theory deviates from classical economic theory, using the argument that externalities in the market prevent the achievement of Pareto optimality. Let's look at some of the externalities that have an impact on housing in a tourism community.

A tourism community exists because it holds an attraction that makes tourists want to visit it. This attraction may be natural or man-made. Disney World in Orlando, Florida, is a classic example of a man-made attraction. The site is flat and devoid of beaches. In fact, much of it was swampland. Without the construction of Disney World and other attractions, there would be very little reason for a tourist to visit the area. There would certainly be no reason for an extensive number of tourists to visit the area.

In contrast to the man-made attraction of a Disney World, consider the beach or mountain tourist destination. The attraction is nature and a natural setting. Tourism development and use of the area must include consideration of the site's natural setting. Many tourism communities have a complex set of rules and regulations designed to preserve their natural setting while allowing for tourism activities. These rules and regulations are externalities imposed on the market, and they can lead to the failure of the housing market.

Regulatory Externalities

Land-use and zoning regulations restrict the type of building that may be constructed in an area. These regulations tend to designate areas for single-family housing use, multifamily housing use, and commercial and industrial use. They also designate minimum lot sizes, minimum setbacks, minimum distances between units, and maximum land coverage for a site (e.g., restricting the percentage of the site that can be built on). Land-use and zoning regulations remove potentially developable land from the market.

The empirical literature contains extensive evidence of market failure in housing markets as a result of externalities. An empirical study by Stephen Malpezzi and Richard Green in 1996 found that the housing markets function efficiently in markets without excessive regulation but function inefficiently in markets with excessive regulation. Excessive regulation results in an ownership externality and negative external costs to the owners. Malpezzi and Green examine the externality of excessive regulation as a cause of market failure and the effect this externality has on the supply and cost of housing. They divide housing into standard quality and low quality, presuming that the cost of the two should differ as a result of quality differences, and they examine the hypothesis that excessive regulation alters the supply and cost of low-quality housing. They find that the bottom of the housing market functions efficiently when allowed to, but it functions inefficiently when excessive regulation exists; that "overly stringent local land use regulations," such as growth controls and building permit moratoria, lead to price increases in the cost of low-quality housing relative to the cost of standard housing, decreased production of low-cost housing, and tighter vacancy rates (Malpezzi and Green 1996, 1817).

Land-use regulations were found to be "the most significant market intervention undertaken by state and local governments," in a study by Eric Hanushek and John Quigley (1990, 176), which also noted that most of the land-use planning in the United States is adopted by small units of government, often without regard for the impacts on the broader region.

Katz and Rosen (1987) note that development restrictions have the effect of raising housing prices because the cost increases associated with the regulations cause the housing developers to focus on the production of more expensive dwelling units; Pendall (2000) concludes that low-density zoning regulations act to shift production away from rental and low-end units and toward more high-end units.

A study in 2002 by the Brookings Institution, the Washington D.C. think tank, found that land-use and zoning regulations have the effect of raising the price of housing by limiting the supply of affordable housing and excluding lower-income households (Nelson et al. 2002, 2).

In a tourism community, these regulations may be used to restrict the development of properties not in character with the perceived tourism community goals. There may be height restrictions on properties so as not to destroy the views of natural resources (such as the mountains or the ocean), or there may be regulations restricting any changes that would alter the quaintness of the village or the historic character of the community.

Land-use and zoning regulations restrict what owners may do with an individual piece of property. Owners may be restricted to using the property for residential rather than commercial purposes. They may be able to construct a single-family dwelling on the property but not construct a duplex or multiple-unit dwelling. The single-family dwelling may have minimum or maximum size requirements. The ability to use all or a part of a site for smaller, more affordable housing may also be restricted. Owners may be allowed to construct an in-law apartment or guest house on the property, but they may not be able to build the same structure strictly for the purpose of rental to tourists or unrelated third parties. Zoning and land-use regulations present an ownership externality, with the external costs imposed on the owners.

Building codes may be imposed to increase the perceived quality of the housing. These codes establish minimum standards for the construction and rehabilitation of buildings. As has been identified in many U.S. cities, building codes can affect the rehabilitation of older buildings by imposing standards that are very difficult to meet. Building codes may act to increase the cost of the housing, while also increasing the quality.

Tourism communities may also use visual impact regulations in an effort to restrict development. Specifically, these regulations may be used to restrict development that would negatively affect the tourism business. Many tourism communities strive to present an image of paradise. Shantytowns and substandard housing within the view of tourist hotels may not project the desired image, and may be regulated away. Tourists may not want to look out the windows of their resort hotel and see a series of high-rise buildings between the hotel and the ocean. Visual impact regulations are ownership externalities, although they may also be public-good externalities when the regulations are primarily designed to protect the overall tourism economy.

Shucksmith (1981) notes that development activities fail to take into account the landscape and amenities of the local community, and that development restrictions are necessary to preserve these community assets. Without development restrictions, second-home development in rural areas can destroy the physical characteristics of the community.

Many tourism communities have imposed growth-limiting regulations. These regulations may take the form of limitations on the amount of growth allowed in any period (measured, for instance, in new hotel rooms or new housing units), or they may take the form of limiting the available land that can be developed. Growth-limiting regulations may also be known as growth caps, growth controls, or growth management. These regulations are ownership externalities. When the growth-limiting regulations restrict the supply of land, they have the effect of increasing housing prices, often significantly, while growth-limiting regulations that do not restrict the supply of land have a much smaller effect on housing prices (Nelson et al. 2002).

Topographical Constraints

Environmental regulations affect where and what type of development can take place. For instance, environmental regulations may prohibit the development of housing on beaches or mountainsides to minimize environmental impact, even though it is technologically possible to build on these locations. When the restrictions on the development of beaches and mountains are for public purposes (e.g., to limit pollution or to preserve natural resources, such as forests or barrier reefs), a public-good externality is created. The restrictions on development may also be an ownership externality when the restrictions result from the desire of others to maintain the land without extensive development.

Environmental regulations resulting from natural resource limitations, such as limited fresh water availability, limits on sanitation or the ability to dispose of waste products, and air quality regulations, are externalities that restrict development and increase the cost of housing (Malpezzi and Green 1996).

The Second-Home Externality

A final externality that exists in tourism communities is the second-home owner. Nick Gallent and Mark Tewdwr-Jones describe second-home owners as "external sources of competition" (2001, 60). These home buyers are economically based in another market, but they compete with the locals (the internal economy) in a tourism community housing market for the available housing units.

Second-home ownership is an externality unique to tourism communities. The second-home owner owns housing in the tourism community that he uses as a second home, while maintaining a primary home elsewhere. Second-home owners tend to be wealthier people from another housing market who use their house in the tourism community part-time or seasonally. Second-home owners are unique in several ways. First, their wealth and income is derived from a market other than the tourism community in which they have a second home. For example, many of the second homes in the U.S. Virgin Islands are owned by corporate executives and other wealthy people from mainland U.S. cities. Their wealth is not directly received from the economy of the U.S. Virgin Islands (Mills 1995). Second, the second-home owner tends to purchase housing of high quality, either large and with many features or on prime tourism land, such as on the water or with a view of the mountains or ocean (Mills 1995). This is a technical externality, as it alters the market incentives.

Once again, empirical research identifies the impact second-home demand has had on housing prices in tourism communities. Gallent and Tewdwr-Jones (2000) conducted an extensive study of rural second-home ownership in Europe and its impact on the housing market; they found that second-home buyers tend to originate from economies external to the tourism community in which the home is purchased, and they concluded that as second-home ownership increases in a community, inflationary pressure is put on housing prices, often to the extent that housing is no longer affordable to locals. In addition, Shucksmith (1981) cites the significant gap that may exist between urban and rural incomes, with urban incomes being significantly higher. Income from the external urban economy is used to purchase second homes in the lower income area, increasing housing prices and removing housing units from the local market but not generating an increase in local wages.

Determining If Market Failure Exists

Bator identified externalities as the causes of market failure. As discussed above, subsequent researchers have identified many externalities unique to the housing market, such as zoning regulations, land-use regulations, building codes, environmental regulations, visual-impact regulations, growth-management regulations, and enough second-home ownership to have an economic impact, which is unique to the tourism community.

A condition of market failure is the existence of externalities. The empirical literature demonstrates that significant externalities can exist in the housing sector of tourism communities. The economic theory of market failure applies when housing problems in tourism communities are associated with externalities, and the externalities cannot be removed.

The final step in analyzing the housing market in tourism communities for market failure is the rejection of alternative hypotheses as the cause of the problem. If the housing problems are not caused by externalities, and the solution is not intervention, what other solutions are possible?

There are essentially two solutions when the housing market in tourism communities is not functioning efficiently. If we assume that externalities caused market failure, the solutions lie in interventions. The community intervenes to supply the housing the market does not provide, or the community acts to modify or remove the externalities that affect housing. If we do not assume externalities caused the market failure, the solution lies not in market intervention but in market forces. The disequilibrium of the market is corrected through Adam Smith's invisible hand.

As discussed above, many externalities can be considered unique to tourism communities. While zoning regulations, land-use regulations, and building codes are common to many housing markets, many environmental regulations, growth limitations, and visual-impact regulations are more prominent in tourism communities. Environmental regulations affecting coastal areas or mountain ranges are very likely to have an impact on tourism communities simply because many tourism communities are located along the beach or in mountainous areas. Second-home ownership tends to concentrate in tourism communities. Visual-impact regulations are often an important means of maintaining the quaintness and other characteristics of an area that attracts tourists. The snow-covered village of a mountain resort could be torn down and replaced by a shopping mall, or the view of the ocean could be restricted by the construction of high-rise buildings. These actions, however, would destroy an element of what attracts tourists to the tourism community.

An intervention would be necessary to remove the externalities. If the externalities were removed, some, if not all, of the characteristics that made the market attractive for tourism might also disappear. Additionally, some of the environmental regulations dealing with public goods might be impossible to remove without overall harm to the community.

In a market where tourism workers and community residents cannot afford housing, classical laissez-faire economics would call for adjustments in supply and demand until equilibrium is reached and Pareto optimality achieved.

The chief problem identified with housing in tourism communities is that tourism workers and community residents cannot afford it. Regulations (externalities) restrict the supply of housing and alter the housing cost structure, making it more profitable for housing entrepreneurs to supply more expensive rather than less expensive housing. The wages of the tourism workers and community residents are such that they cannot afford (or demand) the housing that is being supplied. The regulatory structure is such that the housing being demanded cannot be supplied.

If the problem is not market failure but wages or the relationship between wage levels and the cost of housing, then one of the solutions would be to increase wages. The wage increase should be large enough to enable workers and residents to afford housing in the market. As identified by Mills, there may be a substantial gap between existing wages and existing fair market rents and housing prices. Significant wage increases may be necessary (Mills 1995).

The tourism industry requires labor to operate. If wages are increased, the prices for tourism goods and services must also increase. If wages are significantly increased, significant price increases must also occur. If tourism demand for a given location is elastic, price increases will have the effect of decreasing tourism demand for that location. That decreasing demand will lead to a decrease in tourism suppliers, which will lead to a decrease in the demand for workers, which in turn will lead to a decline in wages. Thus we see that tourism demand is price sensitive. If tourism prices are increased in only one tourism location (which has externalities affecting housing prices), tourism demand will decline in that location. Ultimately, the tourism community becomes smaller. The community will need other industries to replace tourism. But many beach and mountain communities have developed tourism as an alternative to agricultural and primary materials economies. A decrease in tourism demand could lead to a decline in the wealth of the community. Therefore, an increase in wages in a tourism community (with externalities affecting housing prices) could be expected to lead to a decline in tourism demand, followed by a decline in wages.

Alternatively, instead of increasing wages, the tourism business could intervene in the market and supply housing or provide financial subsidies for housing. The tourism business would intervene when it becomes more cost effective to supply the housing or provide the subsidy than to continue to increase wages. As in the case of wage increases, however, the costs of this alternative would be borne by the tourism businesses, and therefore this alternative could be expected to have an effect similar to wage increases: increased prices in the market, followed by reduced tourism demand. Tourism businesses would pursue this alternative only to the extent that the benefits exceeded the costs.

Is market failure theory applicable to housing markets in tourism communities? The theoretical foundation presented here shows that (1) a linkage exists between externalities in the housing markets and market failure theory, (2) intervention is necessary to remove the externalities, (3) some of the externalities may in fact not be removable, and (4) free-market mechanisms may not be effective in solving the housing problems in tourism communities. The market has failed, and intervention is necessary.

Larry Bourne, in his book *The Geography of Housing*, summarizes the housing and market failure debate: "The crux of the debate is the ability or inability of the private market to adequately provide housing for all. Few would now subscribe to the view that it can do so" (1981, 171).

7

When Market Failure Occurs

Economic theory identifies the existence of externalities in a community as a condition that can lead to the failure of the local housing market. But externalities exist in many communities and the housing market has not failed in all of them. The key is to distinguish instances in which market failure will occur from those in which it will not occur. This chapter describes the instances in which externalities lead to market failure and discusses the need for interventions to address those failures.

Community Housing Crisis

What specific effect do the externalities of land-use, zoning, and growth-management regulations, topographical and environmental constraints, and second-home demand have on housing costs in a community?

The answer depends on other factors, notably the availability of housing in an adjoining community that can be substituted for housing in the subject community. In economics this is called the elasticity of market demand—the ability or inability of those seeking housing to shift to another community. The elasticity of market demand is the key factor affecting housing prices. If another location cannot be substituted (inelastic demand), high housing prices will occur in the community (Nelson et al. 2002). If another community can be substituted, the increase in housing prices is likely to be less severe. This is a key consideration for tourism communities. Are there adjoining communities where housing costs are more affordable and from which workers can commute to their places of employment, or is the community constrained in some way, such as by mountains or water, so that comparable substitute communities do not exist? For many tourism communities, including those presented in this book, because of their unique natural attractions and topographical constraints, substitute housing is not available.

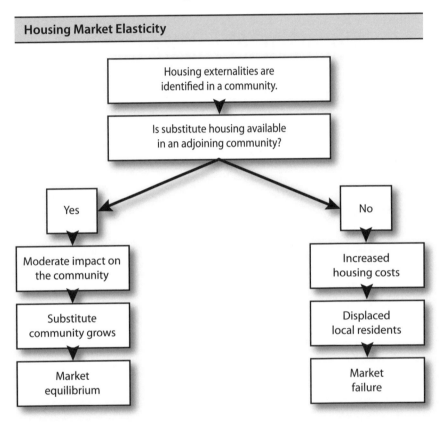

Housing Market Elasticity

Housing externalities are identified in a community.

Is substitute housing available in an adjoining community?

Yes

No

Moderate impact on the community

Increased housing costs

Substitute community grows

Displaced local residents

Market equilibrium

Market failure

Second-Home Demand

In a tourism community, second-home demand has a significant influence on housing prices and economic activity. When an excess housing supply exists, and second-home demand supplements local demand, second homes are beneficial to the community. But second-home demand ceases to be a benefit and becomes a burden when an excess housing supply does not exist and second-home buyers displace local residents and cause housing prices to increase beyond the means of local residents (Shucksmith 1981; Gallent 1997). High second-home demand in tourism communities results in house price inflation and a decline in housing opportunities for the local residents. Local residents with lower incomes are unable to compete with more affluent second-home buyers for the available housing units (Bollom 1978; Shucksmith 1981; Mills 1995; Gallent and Tewdwr-Jones 2000, 2001). A community housing crisis develops.

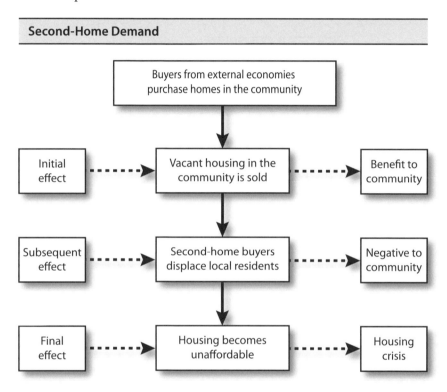

Land-Use and Zoning Regulations

The imposition of land-use and zoning regulations constrains housing construction, limiting the opportunity for development and adding costs to the development process. As a result of these increased production costs, housing developers shift production away from less expensive housing units toward more expensive housing units, where the increased costs can more easily be recovered (Katz and Rosen 1987; Malpezzi and Green 1996; Pendall 2000; Nelson et al. 2002). In practice, land-use and zoning regulations, which rely solely on the market, often lead to a complete absence of affordable housing development as developers create only more expensive housing units. In contrast, growth-management regulations can contain provisions for the development of affordable units, and have been found to be more effective in generating affordable units (Nelson et al. 2002).

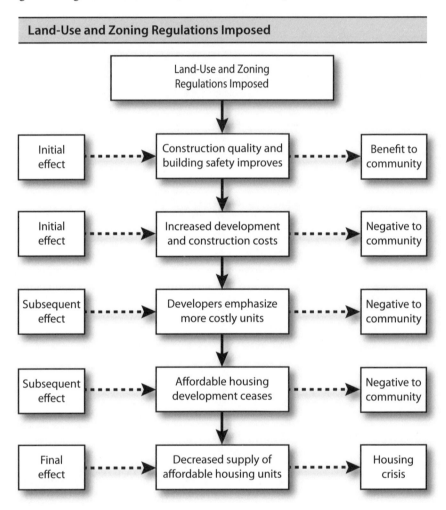

Growth-Management Regulations

Increased housing costs have been identified as one of the primary consequences of growth-management controls and land-use and zoning regulations. Growth-management regulations act to control the amount of development that can take place in a community, thereby controlling the negative effects of development. Growth-management regulations may be imposed to limit population growth, to limit residential or commercial development, to preserve open space, and to limit environmental degradation. Growth-management controls lead to an increased quality of life in the community, making it a more desirable place to live and leading to increases in housing prices as housing demand increases (Nelson et al. 2002). Overall, housing prices are 17 percent to 38 percent higher in communities with growth-management regulations than in communities without those regulations (Katz and Rosen 1987).

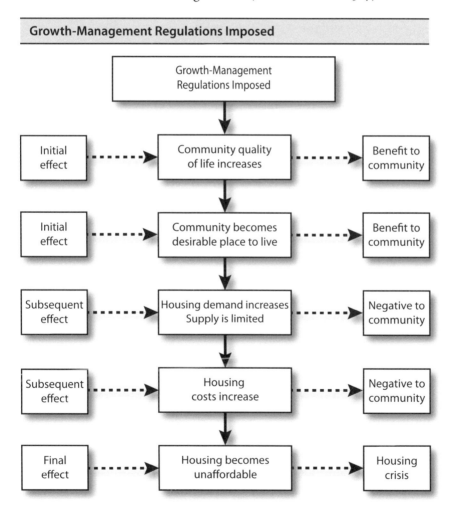

Growth-Management Regulations Imposed

Environmental and Topographical Constraints

Environmental constraints, such as limitations on available fresh water, limits on sanitation capacity, and clean air requirements, were found to restrict development opportunities and lead to increased housing prices (Malpezzi and Green 1996). Significant topographical constraints, such as bodies of water that reduce usable land, beach area, dunes, and mountain terrain, were identified as factors that can increase housing and land prices by up to 40 percent (Rose 1989).

Housing Intervention

When market failure occurs, an intervention is necessary to provide what the market does not provide. In the context of a housing market failure, an intervention is necessary to provide the housing not provided by the market. Exhibit 2 shows the classic theoretical model of housing market invention. For my revised theoretical model, see Exhibit 1 on page 31.

Theory

The literature identifies the elements of an intervention. When a housing market failure occurs in a tourism community, a housing crisis occurs and is indicated by resident complaints to local government regarding housing costs. At this point, the government chooses to intervene or chooses, consciously or unconsciously, not to intervene. If resident complaints are ignored, an intervention does not occur, and the market failure continues. If the government does intervene, both policy support and program funding are needed for a successful intervention (Shucksmith 1981; Gallent and Tewdwr-Jones 2000).

The housing literature notes two types of interventions that have been successful in mitigating market failure conditions in tourism communities: the direct public provision of housing units, and actions on the part of the government and public agencies that enable the private provision of housing units. While the direct public provision of housing units has been the more common approach to housing interventions, the recent literature emphasizes public entities assuming the role of enablers for affordable housing construction rather than the role of direct builders (Shucksmith 1981; Gallent and Tewdwr-Jones 2000).

The housing literature also identifies the lack of success communities have had in controlling second-home conversions, citing difficulty in controlling sales to second-home owners and in enforcing occupancy restrictions once the unit has been sold (Gallent and Tewdwr-Jones 2001).

A History of Intervention

History is full of examples of businesses and communities acting to provide housing for workers. The mid-nineteenth century saw the beginning of the so-called company towns in northeastern sections of the United States as the textile industry began to develop and it became necessary to attract workers from rural areas to the developing mill towns. To attract and retain workers, mill owners often built and owned the housing in which the workers lived. The downside, from the workers' perspective, was that their housing was linked to their employment, and if they quit or were fired, they could immediately find themselves in need of new housing as well as a new job.

As the industrial revolution moved to the steel, manufacturing, and mining centers of the Midwest and Appalachia, the growing businesses in these regions also looked to provide housing for their workers. The same phenomena was observed in the mining towns of the Rocky Mountains during the later part of the nineteenth century. The existence of readily available business-owned housing helped to assure a supply of miners for the mines, and created an incentive for the miners to stay employed with the company that supplied the housing (Crawford 1995). In the twentieth century, developing nations used the provision of worker housing as a means of attracting workers from rural areas to the developing industrial areas, repeating the experiences of the nineteenth century in the United States (Burns et al. 1977).

More recently, within the United States and Western Europe, the model has moved from one in which the employer supplies housing to one in which the community and community groups act to supply housing. For example, in Britain, the employers and in large part the government have begun to withdraw from the business of providing housing for workers, selling off existing housing units to current residents; and they have begun to rely on a network of voluntary and nonprofit organizations to provide affordable housing (Doogan 1996; Gallent and Tewdwr-Jones 2000). In Boston, Massachusetts, one of the most expensive housing markets in the United States, the hotel and restaurant workers union

Exhibit 2. – Theoretical Model of Housing Market Intervention

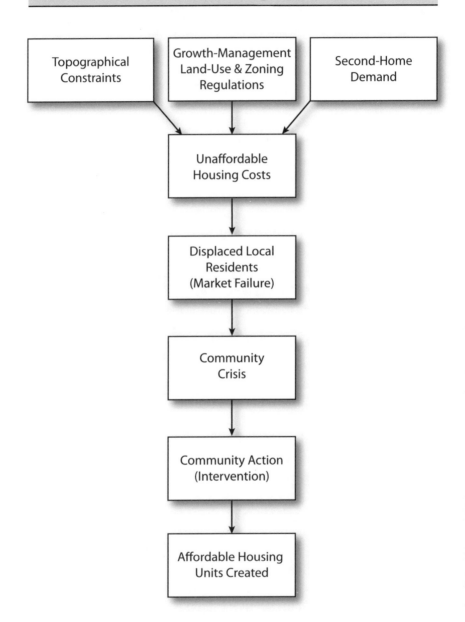

has forced modification of the labor laws to allow union pension funds to be made available as housing funds for the primarily low-wage union members in support of efforts to increase home ownership among these families (Ferlauto 1991).

Housing and the Tourism Worker

When considering housing needs in a tourism community, it is important to understand the characteristics of the various groups of tourism workers because the housing requirements differ for each group. In a series of articles based on research at destination resorts in Hawaii, Patricia Adler and Peter Adler (1999) define four classes of tourism workers. First are the "new immigrants," who occupy jobs at the lowest level and for the lowest wages within the tourism businesses, such as housekeeping and grounds maintenance. New immigrants typically arrive from other less developed countries, seeking economic opportunity for themselves in the tourism business, and expanded opportunity for their children. New immigrant tourism workers typically live in housing with many other families to reduce expenses, or they may live in dormitory-style housing provided by the employer.

The second primary group of tourism workers are the "locals." The locals, native to the area, work in lower level tourism jobs, often in jobs just above those held by the new immigrants. The locals, as described by Adler and Adler, are less hard working than the new immigrants, value leisure more, may live with their parents to avoid paying rent, and face high rental costs in the market when they do not live with family. "Seekers," the third identified group, are also new immigrants to the tourism community, but unlike the first group of new immigrants, they do not come from a less developed country but from the mainland and other non-tourism areas of the country. They come seeking recreation and leisure, and they become employed in the tourism business as a means of economic support for their leisure activities. Seekers tend to have more education and more skills than locals or new immigrants, and hence demand higher pay. The seeker group is further subdivided into those workers who are transient, moving from one resort destination to another in search of different leisure experiences; those who intend to stay a short time before pursuing a professional career or while taking time off from a professional career; those who stay for a significant period, such as five to ten years; and those who ultimately become permanent residents of the community. Seekers often exhibit the same housing patterns as the new immigrants, living many people to a unit or relying on the employer to supply housing.

The final tourism worker group identified are the "managers," the resort professionals who make their living in the tourism industry, and often move from resort area to resort area in search of advancement or in response to promotion by their employers. The managers are the most skilled and earn the highest pay, have the most stable and affluent lifestyle of the worker groups identified, and can afford to spend the most for housing.

The Need for Intervention
The availability of affordable housing for low-wage and entry-level workers remains a key factor in attracting and retaining them. When affordable housing is unavailable, a shortage of low-wage and entry-level workers is likely to result. Likewise, when low-wage workers do not have access to the financial and credit markets necessary to finance housing, housing is difficult to obtain, and a shortage of workers can be expected (Belcher and Rejent 1993).

A vibrant tourism economy requires many classes of workers, including many who are paid relatively low wages. As it did in the mining towns of the 1880s, the attraction and retention of workers depends in large part on the availability of housing that workers at all wage levels can afford.

When the market fails to provide this housing, the community must intervene to provide it. In the following pages, Part 3 presents case studies of three tourism communities that have intervened in the market to provide housing for tourism workers and community residents, and one tourism community that has not yet intervened. The cases present the market failure conditions in the communities, examine the interventions that have taken place, and describe the motivation for these interventions.

Part 3
Community Case Studies

8

Aspen, Colorado:
A Pioneer in Resident Housing

Aspen is a winter and summer recreation community located in the Roaring Fork Valley of Colorado, approximately 200 miles southwest of Denver. The greater Aspen area consists of the city of Aspen and some of the surrounding unincorporated areas of Pitkin County. According to the 2000 U.S. Census, Aspen has a population of 5,914, and Pitkin County has a population of 14,872. The city has grown through the annexation of developing areas of the unincorporated county. Aspen is governed by both city and county government, and both entities have been active in addressing housing issues for local residents.

Aspen is bounded on three sides by the Rocky Mountains. Numerous mountain peaks in the Aspen area exceed 14,000 feet. These mountains effectively restrict most ground access to Aspen. The Roaring Fork River runs northwest from Aspen toward Glenwood Springs, and the Roaring Fork Valley represents the only ground access to Aspen that does not run through the mountains. The primary route to Aspen is via Highway 82, which runs northwest from Aspen to Glenwood Springs and then joins Interstate Highway 70. Highway 82 is a four-lane road from Glenwood Springs to the Aspen town line, where it narrows to two lanes. Southeast of Aspen, Highway 82 crosses over Independence Pass, a 14,000-foot narrow winding mountain road that offers access to Aspen from the south and east during the warm seasons only; the mountain roads close down with the first winter snow.

The central town area of Aspen is laid out in a grid running from southeast to northwest on the flat land between the mountains. The central town area contains the downtown commercial center and numerous neighborhoods with housing. It takes approximately ten minutes to walk from one end of the downtown area to the other. Beyond the central town are rural areas with ranches, some housing developments, and the mountains.

In 1877, the silver-mining town of Leadville, to the east of Aspen, and on the other side of the mountains, was the second largest city in Colorado, with a population of 15,000. Aspen's first settlers were gold and silver prospectors who arrived in 1879 from Leadville, traversing the Rockies at Independence Pass. By 1885, Aspen had a population of 4,484, more than 1,000 homes, and active commerce that included mining, transport, and retail. Aspen's population peaked at 10,000 in 1891, and rapidly declined following the collapse of the silver market in 1893, falling to only 1,000 persons by 1910 (Barlow-Perez 2000).

Key events in Aspen history	
1877	First miners arrive
1891	Population peaks at 10,000 persons
1893	Silver market collapses
1910	Population falls to 1,000 persons
1930s	First ski lifts installed
1950s	Summer music festival and Aspen Institute established
1976	Growth-management regulations implemented
1979	Affordable housing units numbered 327
1989	Affordable housing units numbered 741
1990–2002	1,196 additional affordable housing units developed
2002	Affordable housing units numbered 1,937
	Affordable units house 64 percent of population

Aspen's second life began with the ski industry in the late 1930s, when the first ski lifts were installed. A series of ski competitions were soon held that provided national and international exposure for the community, and established Aspen as a world-class ski area. The development of the ski industry in Aspen had two beneficial side effects. Lodging businesses in the downtown area, which had been in disrepair since the mining days, were revitalized by tourism; and a number of wealthy people who were familiar with Aspen's amenities became community benefactors. The businessmen were looking for ways to expand the tourist season beyond the winter months, and several of the wealthy people saw Aspen as an ideal location for cultural programs. During the 1950s, these elements led to the establishment of several summer programs: the Aspen Institute think–tank was started; the Aspen Music Festival was created; and numerous art, music, and photography schools were founded (Barlow-Perez 2000).

Aspen Research

Aspen was selected as a case site for this study after a review of published material from local newspapers, including the *Aspen Times* and the Aspen Daily News, and through a reference in the book *Managing Tourism Growth: Issues and Applications* by Bosselman, Peterson, and McCarthy (1999). Each of these sources indicated that Aspen was a tourism community thought to be a leader in creating affordable housing units for community residents.

Primary, secondary, and interview data were collected on Aspen. Primary data came from the United States Census; secondary data came from newspapers, books, and community publications such as strategic plans and housing program guidelines. Guided semi-structured interviews were conducted with six key informants in Aspen: the head of the housing authority, the community development director, and four community and political leaders. Interview questions were designed to probe the expertise and experience of the respondents so as to gather data about housing in Aspen and about local events and actions that have affected the housing market.

Aspen uses the terms "free-market housing" and "affordable housing" to describe the city's different classes of housing units. Affordable housing units are those that can be purchased or rented only by individuals or families who meet income, residency, or work location restrictions associated with the units (i.e., work in Aspen/Pitkin County, live in Aspen/Pitkin County, or have an income within specified ranges). Free-market housing units are those that do not have any restrictions on who may buy or rent them. An understanding of the distinction between free-market housing and affordable housing is critical to understanding housing in Aspen.

Tourism

Today, Aspen's economy depends heavily on tourism. According to figures from the 2000 U.S. Census, close to half of the employees in Aspen/ Pitkin County work in tourist-related jobs. In Colorado and nationally only a little more than a tenth of employees work in the same kinds of jobs. Direct tourism employers consist of the ski, lodging, restaurant, and retail industries. Indirect tourism employment includes the service industries that support the tourism businesses, and service businesses such as construction and home maintenance that support the second homes in Aspen. Using table 8–1, you can compare Aspen's employment by industry with that of Colorado and the United States.

During the winter, skiing and other winter sports are the primary tourist activities in Aspen. During the summer, education and recreation activities drive the economy. Education programs in Aspen during the summer months include art, music, and literature schools. Recreation includes outdoor activities on the mountains and the trails surrounding them.

Aspen is located a significant distance from Colorado's population centers. The drive time from Denver is four hours. Commercial air travel to Aspen is limited, with only six flights a day from Denver; and it is expensive relative to the cost of flying to Denver and other nearby cities. As a result, most tourists who travel to Aspen stay for an extended period. Day-trippers are not a significant part of Aspen's tourist economy.

The tourism workers in Aspen include members of each of the four groups identified by Peter Adler and Patricia Adler: new immigrants, locals, seekers, and managers (1999). (See chapter 7 for a full description of the groups.) The interviews revealed that many of the local residents had come to Aspen originally as seekers and chose to remain and become permanent residents.

"It's not uncommon to have a fifty-three-year-old ski instructor in Aspen. They came here when they were in their twenties and thirties."

The interviews revealed that because of the current high cost of living in Aspen, fewer seekers were moving to the town today than in years past. The ski businesses are staffed by local residents and by the so-called Euro locals, Europeans who have come to Aspen specifically to work at the ski resorts. New immigrants arriving in Aspen today are often Hispanic, including undocumented workers, many of whom find employment as service workers supporting the upkeep of the second homes.

Table 8–1. Employment by industry in Aspen, Colorado, and the United States (percent)

	Aspen/Pitkin Co.	Colorado	United States
Tourism employment			
Arts, entertainment & recreation	15.8	2.1	1.5
Accommodation & food services	30.4	10.5	10.2
Total tourism employment	46.2	12.7	11.7
Other employment			
Construction	7.0	8.3	5.8
Real estate & rental & leasing	4.7	2.3	1.7
Retail trade	13.2	13.2	13.0
Finance & insurance	1.9	5.3	5.2
Professional, scientific & technical	5.4	7.3	6.0
Other	21.7	51.0	56.6
Total other employment	53.8	87.3	88.3
Total Employment	100.0	100.0	100.0

Source: 2000 County Business Patterns, U.S. Census Bureau.

Housing Market Failure Analysis

As discussed more fully in Part 2, the imposition of growth-management regulations and land-use and zoning regulations in a community can have a negative effect on housing prices and on the types of housing constructed.

These regulations constrain the number and type of housing units that can be constructed, and lead developers to shift production to the creation of more expensive housing, which is more profitable for the developer, and away from the creation of less expensive housing. Those seeking housing are forced to either pay the increased costs or move to another community.

Additionally, second-home demand, when brought about by buyers from an economy external to the subject community, can have a significant impact on housing costs in the subject community, particularly when the second-home buyer purchases a home that previously housed a local resident or local worker. High second-home demand in tourism communities results in house price inflation and a decline in housing opportunities for the local residents.

Growth-management and land-use and zoning regulations, second-home demand from external economies, and topographical constraints have been identified as externalities that can cause market failure in a housing market. According to the theories presented in the housing and market failure literature, if these externalities are present in Aspen, then the community has the conditions necessary for a housing market failure, with high housing costs and local residents unable to afford housing.

Housing Market

Table 8–2 presents housing affordability and second-home statistics for Aspen, Colorado, and the United States. According to the 2000 U.S. Census, second homes constitute a much greater percentage of Aspen's housing units than is typical for Colorado or the United States. Even more astounding, the 2000 house prices in Aspen are off the census's scale, which tops out at $1 million. The same thing was true in 1990, although at that time the scale topped out at $500,000. Aspen realtor data show an average home price of between $2.7 million and $4.1 million for Aspen in 2002 (Carroll 2002). Census housing price data include both free-market and

Table 8–2. Housing affordability in Aspen, Colorado, and the United States

	Aspen		Colorado		United States	
	2000	1990	2000	1990	2000	1990
Housing units that are second homes	25.7%	23.5%	4.0%	4.3%	3.1%	3.0%
Median household income	$53,750	$37,467	$47,203	$30,140	$41,994	$30,056
Median house price	$1,000,000	$500,001	$166,600	$82,700	$119,000	$79,100
Ratio of house price to household income	18.6	13.3	3.5	2.7	2.8	2.6
Available funds monthly for housing at 30% median household income	$1,344	$937	$1,180	$754	$1,050	$751
Monthly cost for median-priced house	$5,996	$2,998	$999	$496	$713	$474
Excess income / (income gap)	($4,652)	($2,061)	$181	$258	$336	$277
Households paying more than 30% of income for housing	38.4%	41.9%	28.6%	28.6%	26.9%	27.3%

Source: 1990 and 2000 United States Census.

affordable housing units. The realtor data include only free-market units.

Table 8–2 also presents the ratio of house prices to median household income, allowing you to compare the relationship between house prices and income across different housing markets. The table also allows you to compare the money a median-income family has available monthly for housing, assuming this family uses a 6 percent, 30-year mortgage to purchase a median-priced house and pays no more than 30 percent of income for housing. Both of these measures indicate that housing is un-affordable in Aspen and that housing affordability has decreased since 1990. In 2000, the ratio of house prices to income in Aspen was more than five times the ratio for Colorado and more than six times the ratio for the United States. The comparison of money available for housing expenditures with housing costs indicates that a median-income family in Aspen cannot, by a significant margin, afford a median-priced house in Aspen, while in both Colorado and the United States overall, a me-dian-income family can afford a median-priced house. Additionally, in regard to households paying more than 30 percent of their income for housing, Aspen has 34 percent more than the rest of Colorado, and 43 percent more than the United States overall.

All interview respondents believed free-market housing was very expensive in Aspen. This is consistent with the results of the analysis of the primary data.

> *"They (home prices) average $4.1 million. For $1.3*
> *million you get a single-family starter home."*

> *"For the median income, there is no free-market*
> *stuff [houses] at that price."*

The interview respondents identified several factors that they be-lieved affected the cost of housing in Aspen. First, because of its location bounded by the mountains and the desire to keep mountain areas unde-veloped for environmental and recreational use, Aspen has a finite sup-ply of available land, and the demand for this limited supply has caused prices to rise.

In 1976, Aspen established growth-control regulations limiting resi-dential, commercial, and lodging development, with the goal of preserving the environmental and social quality of life in the community (*Pitkin County Housing Authority* 2002). Four of the six interview respondents identified Aspen's growth cap as a factor affecting housing. They thought the growth cap choked the supply of new housing units and led to increased housing prices throughout the town. This finding is consistent with previous empirical findings, cited in the literature, that growth-management regulations lead to housing price increases.

All the interviewees identified growth in the number of second homes as a primary factor affecting the cost of housing in Aspen. The significant factor here is not just the number of second homes but the change in use of the units from primary residences to second homes. The interviewees indicated that Aspen has experienced the conversion of many free-market units from primary residences to second homes. When a property is converted from a primary residence to a second home, bed space in the community that had been available to house local residents is lost.

> *"Second homes are sucking the worker rooms*
> *out of the system."*

Half of the interview respondents think that second-home purchasers in Aspen are very wealthy, that their wealth comes from an economy external to Aspen, and that they view their second-home purchase as an investment. These interview respondents stated that the demand for the second homes is driven by national and international markets, and is not directly related to the local Aspen economy. This too is consistent with previous empirical work, in which external economies were identified as the source of wealth for second-home purchasers.

> *"The second homes are an alternative to park-*
> *ing the money elsewhere. Aspen is attractive*
> *because of growth management. Growth man-*
> *agement protects the investment. It controls*
> *the scarcity."*

Second-home buyers often have sufficient wealth to purchase the houses without mortgages. Unlike the permanent residents they replace, these wealthy second-home buyers do not have the need or the desire to rent rooms in the houses to local residents or to rent the houses when they are not being used. Rooms formerly available for resident housing are therefore removed from the inventory of available housing units.

Summary

Consistent with prior empirical research, the primary data and interview data collected for Aspen indicate that the town's housing market has been negatively affected by externalities. The topographic limitation of the area, the growth-management regulations, and the demand for second homes by buyers from external economies have led to a market failure in housing, as indicated by the apparently complete absence of free-market housing that can be purchased by a typical community resident and by a reduction in the number of resident housing units.

Housing Intervention

As stated earlier, according to the historical housing and market failure literature, when market failure occurs, an intervention is necessary to provide what the market has not provided. Interventions occur when housing has become unaffordable to the local residents, the residents complain to the local government, and the government reacts.

Motivation for Intervention

Questions asked of the interview respondents were designed to probe for the motivations for Aspen's interventions. Several motivations were identified. One interview respondent with significant knowledge of Aspen's history and housing programs identified the proactive recognition of the issues by the early community leaders as the key to Aspen's current housing intervention philosophy. As the cultural centers began to develop in Aspen in the 1950s and 1960s, many of the community leaders were moneyed people from the eastern and central United States, and they had the means and desire to preserve community in Aspen. The institutions established were integrated with the community rather than separated from it.

> *"The enlightened leaders from the east coast, they were starting to save the town. People like Hunter Thompson. These were social innovators; they*

> *were intrigued by the community; rather than*
> *wanting to rape and pillage, they wanted to in-*
> *novate."*

This social innovation during the early tourism development of Aspen helped prevent the community from being destroyed, and established a culture of social intervention. This history of social intervention led to the establishment of Aspen's current housing programs beginning in the 1970s, when a housing crisis occurred. Two-thirds of the interview respondents believed that the current housing programs were driven primarily by a reaction to community events and a need on the part of the tourism businesses. As housing prices increased in Aspen in the 1970s and 1980s, housing became unaffordable to the middle class, the community fabric began declining, and there was community pressure to control growth and to provide housing. The lack of affordable housing began to lead to worker shortages for the tourism businesses, and the provision of affordable housing was seen as a way to protect the community's tourism base.

> *"Real estate values got out of hand for the average*
> *middle-class workers. If it were only the lower-*
> *class workers, then nothing probably would have*
> *been done. Without the middle class, there were*
> *no members of commissions, no PTA members,*
> *and so forth."*

Effect of Intervention

Most community members in Aspen live in affordable rather than free-market housing. According to data from the Aspen/Pitkin County Housing Authority published in a report by Economic & Planning Systems, Inc. (2002), as of 2000, the affordable units consisted of 1,194 ownership and 793 rental units, representing more than 44 percent of the total housing units in the community. These affordable units house approximately 64 percent of the town's permanent population.

Table 8–3. Housing and population in Aspen, Colorado

	Number	Percent
Resident housing units		
Affordable housing units	1,937	44.5
Free-market housing units	1,296	29.8
Total resident housing units	3,233	74.3
Second-home units	1,121	25.7
Total housing units	4,354	100.0
Average persons per units	1.94	
Population		
In affordable units	3,758	63.5
In free-market units	2,156	36.5
Total population	5,914	100.0

Approximately 17 percent of Aspen's affordable housing (327 units) were built or designated as affordable housing before 1979; 21 percent (414 units) were built or designated between 1980 and 1989. The remaining 62 percent (1,196 units) have been built since 1990 (Economic & Planning Systems 2002). Approximately 1,176 affordable housing units were built directly by the housing authority and other local government agencies or nonprofits, and approximately 761 units were built by private developers (Economic & Planning Systems 2002).

During the interviews, respondents were asked several questions to probe the effect of the interventions on the community. Two community leaders and a housing leader responded, stating that both the community and businesses have benefited from the housing interventions. They cited two key benefits to the community from the existence of affordable housing: the continued existence of a community, with density in neighborhoods, the presence of children, economic vitality, and volunteers for community events; and continued community character. The key benefit of affordable housing cited for businesses is the existence of a stable workforce that provides a labor pool from which the businesses can draw and helps keep wages down.

Programs

The Aspen/Pitkin County Housing Authority administers Aspen's affordable housing programs centrally, managing the publicly owned rental units and administering privately owned rental units. The housing authority qualifies prospective tenants for the units, assures that landlords comply with program requirements, and administers the initial sale and resale of ownership units.

Income limits for affordable housing in Aspen range from a low of $26,400 for a single person with no dependents to a maximum of $192,000 for a family of three adults (Pitkin County Housing Authority 2001). The maximum incomes allowed by the Aspen guidelines are significantly higher than the typical federal and state affordable housing income maximums, which usually cap the need for affordable housing at 80 percent of the area's median income; 80 percent of Aspen's median household income of $53,750 is approximately $43,000.

Aspen uses deed restrictions and sale price caps to control the resale of ownership units. The resale price of affordable ownership units is based on a formula that limits appreciation to between 3 percent and 6 percent per year.

The primary sources of funding for affordable housing in Aspen are a 1 percent real estate transfer tax and a 0.45 percent sales tax dedicated to affordable housing. The sales tax generates an average of $950,000 per year, and the real estate transfer tax generates an average of $3.6 million per year, for a total of $4.5 million per year in affordable housing funds. These funds are used primarily for the purchase of land and for the construction of affordable housing (Aspen Interviews September 2002; Economic & Planning Systems 2002).

The private development of affordable housing in Aspen occurs either as a result of mitigation requirements or as a result of development incentives. Aspen's mitigation programs require that private developers and second-home owners replace any resident housing that is lost through renovation, conversion, and new development. Aspen offers development incentives such as exemptions from growth-management quotas, expedited project approvals, and greater density to private housing developments that contain at least 70 percent affordable housing (Aspen Interviews September 2002: Economic & Planning Systems 2002).

Summary

Aspen's housing interventions are consistent with the findings of previous research. The community is involved in the direct construction of affordable housing units, has included the provision for affordable housing units in its growth-management regulations, and acts as an enabler for affordable housing development. The community has reacted to a housing affordability crisis and supported its housing programs politically and financially. Aspen's interventions contain two elements not found in the literature: the active planning for continued resident housing in the community at the beginning of tourism development, and the reacting to a need to protect the tourism-based economy. Additionally, while much of the literature on affordable housing focuses on the needs of lower income community residents, Aspen's housing interventions differ, focusing primarily on middle-class and higher income community residents.

Housing interventions in Aspen

- **Development, with direct construction of affordable housing units**
- **Enablement, with regulations that include incentives for affordable housing units**
- **Planning actively for affordable housing units as tourism developed**
- **Emphasizing middle-class and higher income community residents**

Community Concerns

In spite of the housing interventions that have occurred and the resulting significant percentage of Aspen residents who live in affordable housing, data from interviews and secondary sources indicate that high-cost free-market housing continues to have an impact on the Aspen community.

According to the Aspen Affordable Housing Strategic Plan, the city has established a goal of having 60 percent of the people who work in Aspen also live there, with the belief that this is the critical threshold for a viable community (Economic & Planning Systems 2002). The 60 percent threshold is measured using households with at least one employee working in Aspen as a proxy for people working in Aspen. As of 2002, there were 7,800 households with at least one employee working in Aspen. To achieve the 60 percent target, 4,680 households would need to be housed in Aspen. But as of 2002, only 3,684 households, or 47 percent, were housed in Aspen, including those living in affordable housing and those living in free-market units (Economic & Planning Systems 2002). To achieve its goal, the city needs to increase the number of households living in Aspen by 996, and perhaps increase its population as well.

Five of the six interview respondents expressed concern that the social fabric of the community was at risk without continued affordable housing available in the community. They fear that as more of Aspen's workers commute from the down-valley communities and the quality of life improves down valley, the sense of community that exists in Aspen may be lost.

> *"If you don't have 60 percent, the people will want to live other places. The barbeque, the Little League, the friends, the social events, are in other places."*

Those who work in Aspen but do not live there commute from one of the towns down valley, primarily from Basalt and Glenwood Springs along Route 82 northwest of Aspen, and communities such as Rifle and Eagle, which are beyond Glenwood Springs, more than 40 miles from Aspen. Cars, car pools, and bus service are the primary means of commuting. Two respondents cited as a concern the traffic generated by the commuters and by Aspen residents going down valley to shop.

One community leader cited the affordable housing mitigation charges and development restrictions as having a negative effect on new development in Aspen.

> *"The [mitigation] program stalls commercial development. No new buildings are being built. It is cost prohibitive to tear down and replace some of the 1960s buildings that are obsolete or marginal. The mitigation costs are too high."*

All of the interview respondents cited problems with the existing affordable housing programs, including complexity, expiration of deed restrictions, politicization of the process, and stalled commercial development. Aspen's affordable housing programs were first developed in the 1970s and have been modified over time. Many program restrictions apply only to certain units or do not apply in the same way to all the units, which creates confusion and continued community and political debate (Aspen Interviews September 2002).

> *"The program is dated. It's twenty-five years old."*

> *"Operationally, we need to systematize things so that they are consistent. For example, all the different deed restrictions we have."*

Three interview respondents specifically cited the challenges the affordable housing programs face as people's lives change. Divorce, part-time children, and the need to downsize housing were all cited as events that complicate the administration of the housing programs and affect the allocation of housing units, as were concerns regarding the absence of youth in the community and the inability of many of the younger workers to purchase housing in Aspen. Many residents of affordable housing in Aspen have lived in the city for a significant period; they are aging and nearing an age when they will retire or curtail their working hours. No incentive that would induce retiring workers to vacate Aspen's affordable housing is built into the program, nor is there a mechanism by which empty nesters or retiring workers can downsize units within the affordable housing programs. As a result, retired workers continue to live in affordable housing and place additional stress on Aspen's ability to achieve its housing goals for workers.

Summary of Research Findings

A housing market failure has occurred in Aspen. According to the housing and market failure literature, externalities that cause market failure in housing markets include second-home demand, growth-management regulations, and topographical constraints. The research has identified all of these conditions as present in Aspen, and the data indicate that housing costs are well beyond the means of the typical Aspen resident.

A number of housing interventions have taken place in Aspen, including the public development of affordable housing, and regulations and incentives to facilitate its private development. Significantly, my research has identified several interventions that are consistent with the literature, including reaction to a housing crisis, the public development of affordable housing, the government acting as an enabler for affordable housing development, and political and financial support for the affordable housing programs. My research has also identified several intervention strategies not found in the literature, including active planning for resident housing as tourism development occurs, reaction to a need to protect the community's tourism economic base, and development of programs that focus on middle-income residents.

Additionally, significant community concerns regarding the housing interventions have been identified. Free-market housing units continue to be converted to second homes, placing increased demand on the community's affordable housing programs; the community's population is aging, but affordable housing units are not being vacated and made available to younger workers; and the administration of the affordable housing programs has become complex and at times problematic.

In spite of the concerns identified, Aspen's housing interventions appear to have been successful. The affordable housing programs house 64 percent of residents, a funding mechanism is in place for affordable housing development, affordable housing continues to be built in Aspen, there is community support for the programs, and all interview respondents believe the housing programs have been successful in providing affordable housing for residents and in preserving a sense of community in Aspen. But the community concerns indicate that the externalities affecting the housing market in Aspen are constantly changing and that housing interventions implemented must be constantly reviewed and revised to remain effective.

9

Whistler, British Columbia: Planning for a Solution

Whistler is a winter and summer recreation community located in the Coast Mountains of western British Columbia, approximately 75 miles north of Vancouver. According to the 2001 Canadian Census (Statistics Canada 2001 a), Whistler has a population of 8,896, and the town estimates that the workforce peaks at 13,500 during the prime winter tourism season. Whistler continues to grow, and many experts expect the permanent population to reach more than 14,000 by 2020 (Resort Municipality of Whistler 2003 a).

The only road serving Whistler is Highway 99, a two-lane highway that runs north from Vancouver through the mountains to Squamish, Whistler, and then on to Pemberton. The drive from Squamish to Whistler takes approximately 45 minutes, and the drive from Whistler to Pemberton takes about 30 minutes. Beyond Pemberton, Highway 99 traverses the mountains for 110 kilometers to the town of Lillooet in the Fraser River Valley in central British Columbia.

Whistler is bounded on all sides by mountains. The Green River begins in the mountains east of town and runs north before joining the Fraser River. The Squamish River begins in the mountains west of town and runs south, emptying into Howe Bay near the town of Squamish. The mountains and the development of the ski resort have dictated the layout of Whistler and the surrounding area.

Development of the Whistler area as a tourism destination began in the mid-1960s with the construction of the first ski lifts on the south side of Whistler Mountain. Before that, Whistler existed only as a series of logging camps, where timber was cut and shipped down valley, and as a series of small fishing cottages on the many local lakes. The area was mostly inaccessible during the winter months. The development of the first ski lifts coincided with the construction of Highway 99 from Vancouver, which provided the first paved access to the area (Bosselman et al. 1999; Barnett 2000). Before tourism began to be developed, most of the land in the Whistler area was crown land, meaning it was owned by the province of British Columbia; and it could be sold for development, given to the town, or retained by the province.

The initial ski lifts were located on the south side of Whistler Mountain, south of the current town, in the area known as Creekside. Soon after the first ski lifts came the first seasonal ski cottages and a push for additional commercial and residential development. In an attempt to plan and control development, the government of British Columbia formally established the town in 1975. The Resort Municipality of Whistler, as the town is officially known, was the first resort community designated in British Columbia, an experiment in tourism development and management (Barnett 2000). Whistler's population was estimated to be less than 1,000 at the time of incorporation (Cubie 2000, 90).

Following its incorporation, plans were devised to develop Whistler as a tourist attraction. Crown land north of Whistler Mountain was sold for development as a planned tourist village, including retail establishments, lodging, and restaurants; and ski lifts were installed on the north side of Whistler Mountain. Further ski development occurred to the north of the village on Blackcomb Mountain (Resort Municipality of Whistler 2002; Crosby 2000). In Whistler, people say it is possible to start in the village center, ski all the mountains, and end the day back in the village center.

Key events in the history of Whistler	
1965	Highway 99 from Vancouver opens
1965–66	First ski lifts open
1975	Resort Municipality of Whistler is incorporated
1979	Construction begins on the village of Whistler
1980	First resident-restricted housing is approved
1983	Whistler Housing Society is formed
1997	Whistler Housing Authority is formed
2001	Total number of resident-restricted units reaches 1,163
2004	Whistler growth cap is reached
	Resident-restricted units total 1,431

Whistler Research

Whistler was first identified as a case site for this research through a reference in the book *Managing Tourism Growth: Issues and Applications,* where it was noted that Whistler had established community goals to provide housing for its residents and for employees working in the community (Bosselman et al. 1999, 164).

Primary, secondary, and interview data were collected in Whistler. A series of guided semi-structured interviews were conducted with five key informants in the community. Interview questions focused on eight data categories: community characteristics, tourism, housing, trends affecting the community, programs, costs, program effects, and lessons learned. Primary data included information from the 1996 and 2001 Canadian Census (Statistics Canada 2001 a); secondary data included local community publications such as housing reports, housing strategic plans, community monitoring reports, and articles published in the local newspapers.

Whistler uses the term "resident-restricted housing" to describe its restricted or affordable housing. In this chapter, restricted or affordable housing will be referred to as resident-restricted housing, and unrestricted housing will be referred to as free-market housing. The term "resident housing" as used in this chapter will refer to either resident-restricted housing or free-market housing.

Tourism

Whistler was developed to be a tourism destination, and the town markets itself as one of North America's premier recreation destination resorts. During the winter, skiing and other outdoor mountain sports are the key attractions. During the warmer months, attractions include hiking trails, mountain biking, golf, and water sports on the lakes and rivers. Several provincial parks are located near Whistler.

> *"There is great skiing. You are five minutes from a high-speed lift. It's the best terrain in North America. There is lots of recreation, mountain biking, trails, restaurants, entertainment, bands."*

Hotel occupancy rates are highest during the winter months, averaging 68 percent, whereas during the summer months they average only 43 percent. During the winter of 2000, Whistler averaged almost 12,000 skiers per day; during the summer, more than 81,000 rounds of golf were played on the town's three golf courses (Resort Municipality of Whistler 2001 b). Interview respondents referred to Whistler as a "hot spot." The town, in partnership with Vancouver, has been selected to host the 2010 Winter Olympics.

The Whistler economy depends on tourism. According to the 2001 Canadian Census, Whistler has a higher than average percentage of employment in the art, culture, recreation, and sport occupations, and in the sales and service occupations (see table 9–1). Other occupations, including business, finance and administration, primary industry, and processing and manufacturing, are underrepresented in Whistler's economy (Statistics Canada 2001 a). Seasonal tourism workers compose 28 percent of Whistler's 13,543-person peak winter workforce (Resort Municipality of Whistler 2001 b, 33).

Table 9–1. Employment by occupation in Whistler and British Columbia (percent)

	Whistler	British Columbia
Tourism-related occupations		
Art, culture, recreation & sport	6.9	3.3
Sales & service occupations	38.4	25.6
Total tourism-related occupations	45.3	28.9
Non-tourism occupations		
Management	17.3	10.8
Business, finance & administration	12.4	17.6
Trades, transport & equip. operators	9.8	14.3
Primary industry	2.4	4.2
Processing & manufacturing	0.5	4.8
Other occupations	12.3	19.4
Total non-tourism occupations	54.7	71.1
Total employment	100.0	100.0

Source: Statistics Canada 2001 a, Canadian Census.

The interviews confirmed the importance of tourism to Whistler's economy. Three interview respondents noted that tourism is the most important element in local economy, that all industries in Whistler are directly or indirectly linked to tourism, and that almost all the workers are involved in tourism. Interview respondents used the phrases "extremely important," "highly important," and "it is the thing, everything" to describe tourism in Whistler.

The interviews also revealed that each of the four tourism worker groups identified by Adler and Adler (1999)—new immigrants, locals, seekers, and managers—was present in Whistler and that many members of the new immigrant worker group were of East Indian origin. (See chapter 7 for a full description of the four tourism worker groups.)

Housing Market Failure Analysis
Externalities—the demand for second homes, topographical constraints, growth-management regulations, and land-use and zoning regulations—have an impact on housing costs in tourism communities.

Growth-management controls, while often leading to an increased quality of life in a community, have also been found to lead to increased housing costs. Land-use and zoning regulations have been found to skew new housing development toward more expensive units, which are more profitable for developers. The demand for second homes, driven by buyers from external economies, has been shown to lead to rising housing prices within a community. Additionally, significant topographical constraints have been identified as a factor that can lead to increases in the price of housing and land. And environmental constraints such as limited availability of fresh water or limited capacity for sanitation can also lead to increased housing prices.

If the identified externalities are present in Whistler, then the community has the conditions that have been shown to lead to a housing market failure, with local residents being unable to afford housing.

Housing Market

Analysis of the data shows that housing costs in absolute terms, and relative to income, are more expensive in Whistler than in the rest of British Columbia or in Canada overall. The most recent published data on housing costs and income from the 1996 Canadian Census (Statistics Canada 1996) are presented in table 9–2. The data show that on an absolute basis, housing costs are 64 percent higher in Whistler than in the rest of British Colombia, and 166 percent higher than in Canada overall. The data also show that incomes are higher in Whistler than in the province or in the nation. Analysis of the ratio of average housing costs to average family income shows, however, that even after adjusting for income, housing costs are 38 percent higher in Whistler than in British Columbia, and 66 percent higher than in Canada overall.

The data in table 9–2 also show that the average family in Whistler cannot afford to purchase the average-priced house in the community, assuming that the purchase were to be made with a 6 percent, 30-year mortgage and the family paid no more than the standard 30 percent of income for the mortgage. The average family would require an income 38 percent higher to be able to afford the purchase. In contrast, the average family in British Columbia would require an income only 2 percent higher to purchase the average house in the province, and the average family in Canada can afford to purchase the average house.

Table 9–2. Housing affordability in Whistler, British Columbia, and Canada	Whistler	British Columbia	Canada
Housing units that are second homes	52.9%	n/a	n/a
Average family income	$68,196	$56,527	$42,493
Average house value	$393,610	$239,745	$147,877
Ratio of house value to family income	5.8	4.2	3.5
Available funds monthly for housing at 30% of median household income	$1,705	$1,413	$1,062
Monthly cost for median-priced house	$2,360	$1,437	$887
Excess income or (income gap)	($655)	($24)	$176
Rental households paying more than 30% of income for housing	70.0%	46.9%	43.2%

Source: All data from Statistics Canada, 1996 Canadian Census, except for Whistler percentage of rental households, from Resort Municipality of Whistler 2001 b, and Whistler percentage of second homes, derived from Whistler community data. All amounts in Canadian currency.

Whistler community data indicate that the town's housing prices have increased significantly since 1996, with the average price of a free-market single-family house rising to C$950,000 and the average price of a free-market condo rising to C$460,000 (Resort Municipality of Whistler 2003 b).

The cost of rental housing is also greater in Whistler than in British Columbia or Canada overall. Rental costs are estimated at between C$980 per month for a one-bedroom unit to C$2,211 per month for a three-bedroom unit (Resort Municipality of Whistler 2001 b, 32). Whistler Housing Authority data indicate that 30 percent of renters pay less than 30 percent of their income on housing, 37 percent pay between 31 percent and 40 percent of their income on housing, and 33 percent pay more than 40 percent of their income on housing (Resort Municipality of Whistler 2001 b, 10). Rent expenditure data as a percentage of household income are presented in table 9–2. In total, 70 percent of Whistler renters pay more than 30 percent of their income for housing; that figure is 49 percent greater than the comparable percentage of renters in British Columbia and 62 percent greater than in all of Canada.

Whistler measures its resident, second-home, and tourist accommodations in terms of bed units. A bed unit is defined as "a measure of the quantity of development that is intended to reflect the servicing and facility requirements of one individual" (Samu 2002, 12). A bed unit is effectively the number of people the housing unit or tourist unit can accommodate. As a planned development, Whistler has established a maximum number of bed units that will be permitted in the community. When the cap is reached, no more houses, apartments, second homes, or tourist accommodations will be permitted.

Several factors that affect the cost of housing in Whistler were identified. The first is a growth cap. The bed unit cap is Whistler's growth cap. The town reached the bed unit cap in 2004. Since no additional housing or tourist units will be permitted at that point, the bed unit cap creates scarcity, and prices rise in the face of increased demand.

> *"The big driver is the cap on development. This limits the supply. The whole valley has been zoned. A set number of bed units have been assigned. No increases in development are possible."*

Additionally, Whistler has many wetland areas and steep slopes on the sides of the mountains that cannot be developed even if the bed unit limits under the growth cap were expanded. The growth cap and these physical limitations limit the supply of housing, and as demand for housing rises, the price of housing also rises.

The interview respondents cited several factors that influenced the demand for housing in Whistler. A favorable Canadian to U.S. dollar exchange rate, which has led to an increase in demand for second homes and investment properties in Canadian resorts by U.S. residents, particularly those from nearby Washington State, was cited by two respondents. Additionally, two respondents indicated that because of Whistler's successful marketing efforts, the town has gained a reputation as a good place to be and as a safe investment.

> *"Whistler is so popular among visitors of means. There is demand for a piece of the place."*

> *"Housing in Whistler is recession proof. There is a diversity of dollar sources. The buyers are recession-proof people. There are worldwide dollars in Whistler, from the Pacific Rim, from the U.S. The investors are running to land. The prices are not stalling."*

All interview respondents indicated that growth in demand for Whistler properties had had a negative effect on housing for local residents. As houses are sold to buyers from outside Whistler, rental housing and rental suites in houses are lost. Buyers of means do not have the financial need to rent the houses or suites in houses to local residents.

As of 2001, Whistler had a permanent population of 8,896, consisting of 3,585 households, an average of 2.48 persons per household, and a total of 3,585 dwelling units (Canadian Census 2001). In computing total dwelling units in a community, Statistics Canada uses different methods from those used by the United States Census Bureau. The United States Census counts all dwelling units in the community, whether used as primary residences or as second homes; Statistics Canada counts only occupied dwelling units used as primary residences, excluding vacant units and second homes. Hence, the number of dwelling units in a community as reported by Statistics Canada typically equals the number of households. Whistler data have been used to supplement Statistics Canada data in determining the number of second homes and estimating the number of residents living in resident housing. Data collected by the community indicate that Whistler has 7,605 total residential (non-tourist) units (Resort Municipality of Whistler 2001 b, 5); when combined with the census data, this shows that Whistler has approximately 4,020 second-home units, 53 percent of its total housing units.

During the interviews, the percentage of second-home units in the community was confirmed by the senior planner, who estimated that "non-primary residents are about 50 percent of the housing."

Summary

The primary and interview data for Whistler indicate that the town's housing market has been negatively affected by externalities that have led to a housing market failure. Whistler is experiencing second-home demand from external economies, the absolute cap on growth imposed by the community has been reached, and the area has numerous geographic and environmental constraints that limit the developable land. The housing data indicate that housing is unaffordable to the average Whistler resident and that Whistler has significantly more residents living in unaffordable housing than the rest of British Columbia or Canada; the interview data suggest that local residents are being displaced by second-home buyers.

Housing Intervention

As explained earlier, when market failure occurs, an intervention is necessary to provide what the market does not provide. In the context of a housing market failure, an intervention is necessary to provide the housing not provided by the market. When a housing market failure occurs in a tourism community, a housing crisis occurs, residents complain to local government about the crisis, and the local government and the community chose whether or not to react.

Motivation for Intervention

Motivations for Whistler's housing interventions include recognition during the planning process that workers should live locally, a need on the part of the tourism businesses for workers, and a proactive reaction to a developing housing crisis. As development began, the community leaders and provincial leaders planned for housing in Whistler. Areas of the town were reserved for housing; a warm bed policy, described below, was developed for the village center and surrounding areas; a land bank was set up to reserve land for housing development; and it was decided that an impact fee would be assessed to those commercial developers who did not develop sufficient housing for their planned workforce.

The first leaders of Whistler studied other communities and took action to provide affordable resident housing during the early stages of development. Whistler's first housing land bank and its first resident-restricted housing development were established in 1980 (Maxwell 2000). All of the interview respondents believed that actions by the early community leaders in planning for housing were instrumental in creating the current community.

> *"The founders of the community decided there should be a community here."*

> *"You want people living in the community. You do not want to bus them in from a slum fifty miles away. You need ownership."*

As mentioned above, Whistler instituted a warm bed policy for many of its condominium units in and around the village center. This policy was created in reaction to the events Whistler's leaders observed in other tourism communities, where condominium units in the village centers were being converted to second homes that were used only a part of the year, and the village centers were empty much of the year. Whistler's warm bed policy limits owner's use of the units to a set number of weeks per year and requires the units to be placed in the rental pool for tourists during the other weeks. The intent of this policy is to keep the village center full of tourists and to prevent the conflict between tourism and second homes that occurs in other tourism communities from occurring in Whistler.

Additionally, Whistler reacted to community events. As the town developed, employee and resident housing became a matter of concern. A 1994 study identified the lack of affordable housing as an issue. Housing was needed to support the tourism business. Local residents were unable to afford housing. Local business owners were unable to find a sufficient supply of workers to run their businesses.

> *"The driving force was a 1994 study identifying employee housing, the environment, and transport as issues. One day, the community woke up to the problem."*

Whistler's housing market intervention creates a supply of local workers for the tourism businesses. This is closely linked to the planning of the community. The developers and tourism business operators recognized the need to have local workers. Local workers would lead to higher service levels for the tourists and in turn would provide greater returns to the developers and tourism business operators.

> *"We did not want non-skier employees living in shanty towns. The service level in Whistler is created from people living in the community and participating in the sports. We achieved a core community."*

Effect of Intervention

At the end of 2001, Whistler's 3,585 non-second-home dwelling units included 1,163 resident-restricted housing units, of which 38.2 percent were ownership units and 61.8 percent were rental units (Samu 2002, 10). When you apply the census average of 2.48 persons per household to Whistler's 1,163 resident-restricted housing units, you find that 2,884 persons—approximately 32 percent of Whistler's population—live in resident-restricted housing.

Table 9–3. Housing and population in Whistler

	Number	Percent
Resident housing units		
Restricted housing units	1,163	15.3
Free-Market housing units	2,422	31.8
Total resident housing units	3,585	47.1
Second-home units	4,020	52.9
Total housing units	7,605	100.0
Average persons per unit	2.48	
Population		
In restricted units	2,884	32.4
In free-market units	6,012	67.6
Total population	8,896	100.0

Source: Population figures from Canadian Census 2001.

The resident-restricted housing programs have helped to create a supply of workers for Whistler businesses. This has allowed service levels to be maintained in the community and has kept the costs for tourists down; workers can be paid lower wages because they do not have to purchase free-market housing. Also, because much of the resident-restricted housing in Whistler has been created privately, and many of the larger employers maintain employee dormitories, there is a feeling that the businesses and the community are partners in housing and that both are part of the solution.

Resident-restricted housing units allow the community to continue to exist. Without this affordable housing, workers and community members would have to live in Pemberton or Squamish and commute to Whistler, and the community in Whistler would die off as long-time residents retired or moved.

> *"There still is a community, a sense of community, and a community base. The people who live in employee housing are no different from those who got here twenty years ago."*

Programs

Resident-restricted housing in Whistler has been developed by non-profit and public entities, and by private developers. The town has used several programs to create and preserve resident-restricted affordable housing. When the community was being planned, the experiences of other mountain resort communities such as Aspen and Vail were studied, and their housing problems were analyzed; Whistler's programs were planned to address the problems experienced by the other resorts. To qualify for resident-restricted housing in Whistler, applicants must work or reside in the community at the time the housing is obtained.

Whistler's primary source of resident-restricted housing is private development. The town uses its land-use and zoning regulations to require private developers to develop resident-restricted housing as part of any development. The planning department negotiates employee housing into the zoning applications. In 1980, Whistler's first resident housing development, Tarpley's Farm, was approved for development after negotiations that included the trade of deed restrictions on the properties for zoning approval (Maxwell 2000). Commercial development in Whistler includes an element of resident-restricted housing. The major ski lift developments all include worker dormitories, which the community includes in its counts of resident-restricted housing. Eighty percent of the resident-restricted housing in Whistler has been developed in partnership with private development (Samu 2000). As mentioned earlier, developers who do not include sufficient resident-restricted housing units in their developments are required to pay an impact fee, which is used for the public development of housing units.

Public development accounts for only 20 percent of resident-restricted housing units in Whistler. Of the community's 1,163 resident-restricted housing units, only 12 percent (144 units) have been developed by the housing authority; 8 percent were publicly developed before the formation of the housing authority (Samu 2000). The impact fees paid into the housing fund have been used to develop these units and to pay part of the annual operating expenses of the housing authority.

An important element in the development of Whistler's resident-restricted housing was the significant quantity of undeveloped crown land that existed in the community. The community plan designated the type and location of development that was to occur on this land. As Whistler developed, this crown land was sold to developers for commercial uses and transferred to the community to be used for public purposes, including resident housing. Once this initial land bank had been used, additional land for resident-restricted housing was purchased in the free market, using money from the housing fund.

The Whistler Housing Authority is responsible for the public development of resident-restricted housing and for the administration of all of the community's resident-restricted housing programs. The housing authority was formed in 1997 as the successor to the nonprofit Whistler Housing Society and the W. V. Housing Corporation (Samu 2002, 4).

The community's primary source of funding for the public development of resident-restricted housing is the housing fund. As stated earlier, when property is developed in Whistler for commercial use, the developer is required to either provide housing for the employees directly or pay an "employee service charge" or impact fee to the housing fund, which is then used for housing development or to pay for the operations of the housing authority. In total, the housing fund has leveraged C$6.5 million into 1,100 resident-restricted housing units. As of 2002, all money in the housing fund had been used; Whistler does not plan to replenish this fund; it will rely on private developers to produce the remainder of the units under the cap.

> *"We used employee service charges that developers pay into the fund to build housing, or the developers built the housing themselves. We leveraged C$6.5 million in the housing fund to build 3,500 employee beds."*

Whistler uses deed restrictions and resale price caps to control the affordability of the resident-restricted units. Several deed restriction models have been used. The deed restrictions on the initial developments expire after some period, such as ninety-nine years; deed restrictions on the later developments are perpetual. Resale market value for resident-restricted ownership units is determined by the rate of change in the Vancouver house price index, which Whistler considers to be a more realistic benchmark than free-market house prices in the community itself.

Summary

The literature indicates that typical housing market interventions in tourism communities include public development of affordable housing units and enablement of private development of those units. Whistler uses both these strategies, with an emphasis on using its community development plan and building regulations to force the private development of affordable housing units. Additionally, Whistler's housing interventions include community political support and funding for the housing programs, two elements identified by the literature as necessary for a successful housing intervention. Finally, Whistler's housing interventions include a significant element of planning for resident housing during the planning of the community as a tourism destination—an element that is not found in the intervention literature—and restrictions on use of units in the village center as second homes, an intervention strategy that previous empirical research identified as unsuccessful.

Housing interventions in Whistler

- **Development, with direct construction of affordable housing units**
- **Enablement, with regulations that include incentives for affordable housing units**
- **Active planning for affordable housing units as the community developed**
- **Community political support for affordable housing**
- **Funding made available for affordable housing**

Community Concerns

In spite of the housing interventions that have occurred and the significant percentage of Whistler residents who live in resident-restricted housing, the cost of free-market housing in the community remains a concern. All of the interview respondents indicated that it was becoming more difficult for workers to find affordable free-market housing for rental or purchase in the town, and that as investors and second-home owners acquired free-market properties, units that had traditionally housed Whistler residents were being lost. The lack of available housing for workers with lower paying positions was a community concern.

> *"The trends from the business survey indicate we fall short for seasonal workers. The dorms are all owned by the mountain companies. There is a pressing shortage of housing for these workers."*

Whistler is essentially built out. All the bed units and commercial and lodging space that was planned has been or is about to be constructed. This has generated pressure from the development community and from affordable housing advocates to remove or increase the allowable units under the growth cap.

Whistler has a goal of housing one-third of its workforce within the municipal boundaries. To meet and sustain this goal, the town needs additional resident-restricted housing units; hence the pressure on the growth cap. Projects in the process of development under the current growth cap will add 268 units to Whistler's resident-restricted housing inventory upon completion in 2004. The community has identified a need for an additional 500 seasonal worker units beyond the current growth cap (Samu 2002).

Whistler has also identified the aging of the community's population as a factor that will affect its ability to achieve its housing goals. As the existing residents age and leave the workforce, many are expected to remain in their existing housing. Additional housing will be required for the new workers who replace those who retire. As of 2003, nonworking permanent residents constituted 16.2 percent of Whistler's population. Community projections indicate that by 2020 that figure will have risen to somewhere between 28 percent and 38 percent. Community planning indicates that the growth cap may have to be modified to absorb this significant increase in the nonworking population while continuing current employment levels (Resort Municipality of Whistler 2003 a).

Moreover, because of Whistler's successful bid for the 2010 Olympics, the community must create additional housing and recreation facilities for the Olympic athletes. Crown land south of Whistler has been designated for Olympic housing and is expected to be used later as affordable housing for Whistler residents. Although the successful bid for the Olympics may require modification of Whistler's growth cap, that modification will include incorporation of the additional crown land into the town's boundaries.

All interview respondents indicated that Whistler workers who did not live in town commuted from either Pemberton to the north or Squamish to the south. Morning and evening traffic congestion along Highway 99 was a growing concern. One community leader, who was also a small business owner, expressed concern about the commute to these towns being difficult in bad weather, leading to worker shortages on bad weather days.

Two interview respondents were concerned because Whistler was becoming a middle-aged community, with many core community members at or near retirement age. Many of the early Whistler residents had been operating businesses in Whistler for twenty years, were house rich and cash poor, and were beginning to sell their businesses and houses, and leaving the community for more affordable locations. As these people moved away, community in Whistler was being lost and was not being replaced. If the youth could not afford to live in Whistler, the growth communities would be Pemberton and Squamish, and not Whistler.

Finally, one community leader indicated a growing concern for the sustainability of Whistler's environment and indicated an ongoing community debate concerning the impact of tourism and development on Whistler's environment.

> *"There is environmental degradation, wetlands damage. The use is causing damage. Wetlands and the environment used to be a negotiable item. Now wetlands and other things are more important."*

Summary of Research Findings

The research data indicate that a housing market failure has occurred in Whistler. The research has identified externalities that include second-home demand, significant growth-management and land-use and zoning regulations, and topographical constraints, which the literature cites as conditions necessary for market failure. In addition, the research indicates that housing is unaffordable to most Whistler residents and that local residents are being displaced by second-home buyers.

Several housing interventions have taken place in Whistler. First, during the initial stages of tourism development, the community leaders studied the effects tourism growth had had on housing affordability in other tourism communities, and as a result, included provisions for affordable housing in Whistler's development plan and instituted an impact fee to be used to fund affordable housing development. This finding is significant because it has not been addressed previously in the housing intervention literature.

Whistler also developed a warm bed policy to limit the second-home use of housing units in the village center, a strategy identified by the literature as unsuccessful in other communities. Additionally, as would be expected from the results of prior research, Whistler's leaders have continued to address housing affordability concerns as the community has developed and have continued to develop affordable resident housing units. Consistent with the housing intervention literature, Whistler's housing interventions include both publicly and privately developed housing units, with the community enabling or facilitating development. Whistler's emphasis on private development is consistent with the findings of Gallent and Tewdwr-Jones (2000), who note that more recent intervention techniques focus on enablement rather than on direct public development.

Overall, Whistler's housing interventions appear to have been successful. The resident-restricted housing programs house more than 32 percent of Whistler's population, there is community support for the programs, all the interview respondents indicated that the housing interventions have been successful, and funding and land-use mechanisms are in place to enable the development of affordable units.

Despite the success of the interventions, community members identified significant concerns regarding the community and housing in Whistler, including continued second-home growth, unaffordable housing, and limitations on future development resulting from the growth cap being reached. These concerns indicate that Whistler's housing interventions need to be ongoing as the community evolves and that the current growth cap may not be sustainable if housing affordability continues to decrease.

10

Martha's Vineyard, Massachusetts: Leveraging Local Assets

Martha's Vineyard is an island community located approximately 10 miles off the coast of Cape Cod in southern Massachusetts, about 80 miles from Boston and 250 miles from New York City. Martha's Vineyard comprises the six towns of Aquinnah, Chilmark, Edgartown, Oak Bluffs, Tisbury, and West Tisbury, with a total population of 14,987. Edgartown, Oak Bluffs, and Tisbury are each approximately the same size, with populations of 3,779, 3,713, and 3,755 respectively; and West Tisbury is not far behind, with 2,467 residents. The remaining population resides in the other two towns on the far end of the island (U.S. Census 2000). Collectively, these towns and the tiny island of Gosnold make up Dukes County. Martha's Vineyard is governed by both town and county governments, with some agencies being town specific, such as planning and zoning, and some agencies being county specific, such as the island's housing authority (Commonwealth of Massachusetts 2002).

Martha's Vineyard is accessible only by water or air. There are no bridges to the island. The primary means of access is by ferry from Woods Hole on the mainland of Cape Cod to either Oak Bluffs or the Vineyard Haven section of Tisbury. The Woods Hole ferries operate year-round, carrying passengers, cars, and cargo. Other ferry service runs from New Bedford, Massachusetts. The New Bedford ferry offers year-round cargo service and passenger service in the summer. The airport on the island allows access by private and commercial aircraft.

The original inhabitants of the island, the Wampanoag Indians, farmed, fished, and traded with the neighboring islands and the mainland. During the 1600s, people of European descent began settling in Massachusetts and formed settlements on Martha's Vineyard (Schneider 2000). The European settlers made their living on Martha's Vineyard in much the same way as the Wampanoag Indians, from farming and from the sea. In addition to fishing, boat building and whaling developed as important parts of the island's economy during the colonial years (Carpineto 1998; Schneider 2000).

The first tourists to Martha's Vineyard were offered promises of simple pleasures and the opportunity to forget modern life. In the early and mid-1800s, the island became known for its revivalist meetings. The summer months saw the Vineyard filled with campgrounds where many mainstream and nonmainstream religious groups held retreats (Schneider 2000).

Tourism began to increase on Martha's Vineyard in the mid-1800s when the railroad was built across Cape Cod. The railroad allowed travel from the major east coast cities to the Cape, making access to Martha's Vineyard and the other islands easier. This was followed by significant land development and land speculation on Martha's Vineyard, with the construction of hotels and the sale of building lots to individuals. This initial development boom was followed by a land bust in 1878, and cyclical development thereafter. By the 1930s, summer tourists were commonplace on the Vineyard and were a source of cash for the local economy (Schneider 2000).

The 1990s saw Martha's Vineyard develop into a vacation hot spot. President Clinton and many celebrities began vacationing on the island, which increased its desirability, led to increasing numbers of tourists, and ultimately decreased the affordability of the island's housing.

Key events in Martha's Vineyard	
1600s	First European settlers arrive
Early 1800s	Summer revivalist meetings fill the Vineyard
Mid-1800s	Cape Cod railroad provides access to east coast cities
	Summer tourism increases
1870s	Summer tourism demand sparks land speculation boom
1878	Land bust follows land boom
1930s	Martha's Vineyard recognized as summer tourist place
1990s	Martha's Vineyard becomes a hot-spot tourist destination
2000	Affordable housing conference held

Martha's Vineyard Research

Martha's Vineyard was initially identified as a case site as a result of my participation in the 2000 Martha's Vineyard conference *Preserving Community: Housing Our Island Families,* and was confirmed as a case site through a review of articles published in the online version of the local newspaper, the *Martha's Vineyard Times,* which indicated that the community had implemented several affordable housing programs since the 2000 conference.

Primary, secondary, and interview data on Martha's Vineyard were collected. Primary data included information from the 1990 and 2000 United States Census and from the Massachusetts Department of Housing and Community Development. Secondary data included articles in the local newspapers and material published by the Dukes County Regional Housing Authority and the Island Affordable Housing Fund. A series of guided semi-structured interviews were conducted with key informants on Martha's Vineyard to probe their knowledge about current housing and tourism trends affecting the community and about motivations for the community's housing interventions.

Tourism

Today, Martha's Vineyard remains a tourism hot spot, offering relaxation and recreation to summer visitors. The traditional reasons for visiting Martha's Vineyard—relaxation, the beaches, nature, and the charm of island life—continue to attract tourists.

> *"People come to the Vineyard for the natural amenities, open spaces, beaches, the community itself. There are farmer's markets, the charm; this is a traditional island community."*

Tourism is an important part of the Martha's Vineyard economy. Table 10-1 provides a summary of the island's employment by industry. Direct tourism employment constitutes almost 22 percent of the employment base of the island, more than double the tourism employment rate for all of Massachusetts (U.S. Census 2000). Direct tourism employers on the island include primarily food and lodging businesses, with some arts, entertainment, and recreation. In addition, Martha's Vineyard has significant indirect tourism employment, specifically in the construction industry, whose workers are involved in support of the many second homes on the island (Martha's Vineyard Interviews 2002; U.S. Census 2000). Combined, direct tourism employment and construction make up more than one-third of the island's employment.

Tourists on Martha's Vineyard are generally divided into two categories, day-trippers and extended-stay tourists. Many of the extended-stay tourists stay for several weeks or more during the summer. Martha's Vineyard uses the term "summer people" to refer to those people who come to the island during the summer and stay for extended periods.

A typical day-tripper to Martha's Vineyard would take the ferry to Oak Bluffs or Vineyard Haven; perhaps rent a car, moped, or bicycle; tour the island or spend the day at the beach; and perhaps patronize some restaurants or tourist-oriented shops. According to the interviews and secondary data, the day-trippers add nothing to the local economy and detract from the quality of life on the island. During the summer, the towns and beaches near the ferry docks are full of day-trippers, creating congestion and gridlock. Martha's Vineyard, like its island neighbor Nantucket, steadfastly refuses to install any traffic signals, so traffic flows slowly during the summer months and particularly when the

Table 10-1. Employment by industry in Martha's Vineyard, Massachusetts, and the United States (percent)

	Martha's Vineyard	Massachusetts	United States
Tourism employment			
Arts, entertainment & recreation	2.7	1.4	1.5
Accommodation & food services	19.1	7.7	10.2
Total tourism employment	21.8	9.1	11.7
Other employment			
Construction	15.0	4.0	5.8
Real estate & rental & leasing	2.8	1.5	1.7
Retail trade	20.7	11.4	13.0
Finance & insurance	5.0	7.0	5.2
Professional, scientific & technical	3.6	7.5	6.0
Other	31.2	59.4	56.6
Total other employment	78.2	90.9	88.3
Total employment	100.0	100.0	100.0

Source: 2000 County Business Patterns, U.S. Census Bureau.

ferry arrives. The main island roads go through each of the towns, and island residents cannot go about their lives without getting caught up in tourist congestion. Additionally, many of the tourist-oriented shops and restaurants are believed to be owned by people from off island, so the money from the day-trippers does not circulate on the island (Martha's Vineyard Interviews 2002; Carpineto 1998).

Martha's Vineyard considers the extended-stay tourists to be the core of their economy; Not only do they bring in money but they add culture and diversity to the island.

> *"Second-home people are drivers in the local economy. They employ the landscapers and service help. They buy things on the island. They are an asset. We are talking about the people who stay a week or two or more."*

The island's many summer activities include entertainment and cultural events. Nonprofit fund-raising events are also prevalent during the summer, with the nonprofit organizations often raising sufficient funds for their entire annual budget then. Many businesses depend on the summer people for their profits.

> *"This is a rural place without tourism. Much poorer, a dying place. Tourism is what makes it diverse and cosmopolitan. It holds the economy together. You get seasonal commerce."*

The interviews revealed a substantial new immigrant population on Martha's Vineyard, consisting primarily of Brazilians. According to the respondents, this group works multiple jobs and lives in dense conditions, with many people to a room. Some of the new immigrant group are thought to be undocumented workers. The seeker and manager tourism worker groups identified by Adler and Adler (1999) are underrepresented on Martha's Vineyard. (See chapter 7 for a full description of the tourism worker groups.) Most of the businesses are privately owned, so the need for professional managers is limited, and the island does not offer the leisure experience that lifestyle seekers want. Most of the tourism workers on the island are locals, as are the managers.

Housing Market Failure Analysis

Housing market failure results from the existence of externalities that negatively affect housing supply and demand in the market. Previous empirical research identified second-home demand by buyers from external economies, growth-management regulations, land-use and zoning regulations, and topographical constraints as the externalities that lead to increased housing prices. Growth-management, land-use, and zoning regulations act to limit the supply of housing and lead to increased housing prices, while second-home buyers from external economies use their wealth to bid up the price of housing in a desirable vacation community, and ultimately price the locals out of the housing market.

The elasticity of market demand (the ability or inability of those seeking housing to shift to another community) was also identified as a key factor affecting housing prices.When home buyers' purchase options are restricted to a single community, such as an island community, and a comparable substitute community is not available, high prices can be expected in the subject community.

If these externalities are present on Martha's Vineyard, the conditions exist for a housing market failure, and high housing costs and displaced local residents can be expected. As my research shows, this is in fact the case on Martha's Vineyard.

Housing Market

Table 10–2 presents housing affordability and second-home data for Martha's Vineyard. According to the 2000 United States census, more than half of the housing units on Martha's Vineyard are second homes, compared to only about 3 percent in Massachusetts and the United States. Furthermore, the percentage of second homes on the island has increased by more than 15 percent since 1990 (U.S. Census 1990; U.S. Census 2000).

According to the 2000 census, the median household income on Martha's Vineyard is 11 percent lower than in Massachusetts and 8 percent higher than in the United States, while the median house price on Martha's Vineyard is 64 percent higher than in Massachusetts and 155 percent higher than in the United States (U.S. Census 2000). Table 10–2

Living and Working in Paradise

Table 10-2. Housing affordability in Martha's Vineyard, Massachusetts, and the United States

	Martha's Vineyard		Massachusetts		United States	
	2000	1990	2000	1990	2000	1990
Housing units that are second homes	53.6%	46.4%	3.6%	3.7%	3.1%	3.0%
Median household income	$45,559	$31,994	$50,502	$36,952	$41,994	$30,056
Median house price	$304,000	$195,800	$185,700	$162,000	$119,000	$79,100
Ratio of house price to household income	6.7	6.1	3.7	4.4	2.8	2.6
Available funds monthly for housing at 30% of median household income	$1,139	$800	$1,263	$924	$1,050	$751
Monthly cost for median-priced house	$1,823	$1,174	$1,113	$971	$713	$474
Excess income or (income gap)	($684)	($374)	$149	($47)	$336	$277
Households paying more than 30% of income for housing	31.8%	35.6%	27.8%	31.0%	26.9%	27.3%

Source: 1990 and 2000 United States Census.

also shows the ratio of house prices to household income, an indicator that allows the comparison of relative housing costs across different markets. The ratio of housing prices to household income for Martha's Vineyard is 81 percent higher than in Massachusetts and 139 percent higher than in the United States. Additionally, this ratio has increased by 10 percent for Martha's Vineyard since 1990, indicating that housing was 10 percent less affordable as of 2000 than it was in 1990.

Also presented in table 10–2 is a comparison of the money a median-income family has available monthly for housing, assuming a maximum expenditure of 30 percent of income on housing and the use of a 6 percent, 30-year mortgage to purchase a median-priced house. This comparison indicates that a median-income family on Martha's Vineyard cannot afford to purchase a median-priced house in the community, and would require an income of $75,865 (60 percent higher) to do so. In comparison, a median-income family in Massachusetts and in the United States can afford to purchase a median-priced house.

Local community data also indicate that free-market housing on Martha's Vineyard is expensive. A local real estate index showed that median home sale values had risen from $197,400 in 1989 to $375,000 in 2001 (Ryan 2001, 23); local data also showed that 81 single-family homes had sold for more than $1 million in 2000 and 2001 (Ryan 2001, 24). The interview respondents cited almost no properties remaining on the island at prices below $300,000.

Census data indicated that apartment rental costs were $1,000 per month for a two-bedroom unit, which could be affordable to the island's median-income household. But two interview respondents said that these costs can increase to several thousand dollars *per week* during the summer season; and Martha's Vineyard suffers from a shortage of rental housing, with few multifamily housing developments and a reliance on single-family housing units to serve the rental market. Overall, almost one-third of island renters pay more than 30 percent of their income for housing (U.S. Census 2000; Ryan 2001; Martha's Vineyard Interviews 2002).

All of the interview respondents cited the fact that houses were purchased by people from off island and converted to second homes as the primary cause of the increased house prices and the housing shortages facing island residents. Secondary data revealed that new home construction on the island has focused on second-home owners rather than on island residents. "During the 1990's, Martha's Vineyard added 2,700 seasonal and part-time homes and 1,000 owner-occupied homes" (Ryan 2001, 16).

The interview respondents identified the second-home buyers as wealthy people whose wealth derived from economies external to Martha's Vineyard and who do not need to rent their units, or rooms in their units, in order to pay the mortgage.

> *"This is a resort community. It [housing] is insulated from the market. It is almost always on the upswing. There is no fluctuation based on the economy."*

One community leader indicated that Martha's Vineyard uses its zoning and land-use regulations to control growth and limit the type and character of structures built; the towns on the island have instituted minimum lot-size requirements of several acres for residential development; and they restrict commercial development that does not conform to the character of the island. Martha's Vineyard values open space, has zoned land for agricultural use only, and has set aside land for conservation. Additionally, housing development on Martha's Vineyard is constrained by the physical characteristics of an island community, including a finite amount of land and numerous restricted areas such as wetlands, beaches, and dunes, which cannot be developed.

Finally, the housing market for Martha's Vineyard is not elastic. There are no adjoining communities from which workers can easily or cheaply commute daily. The housing for those who work on the island needs to be located on the island. No affordable substitute housing is available.

> *"You cannot have the fireman living in New Bedford and commuting in. It doesn't work."*

Summary

Consistent with the literature, the data indicate that housing on Martha's Vineyard has been negatively affected by externalities that limit housing supply and by inelastic housing demand, which has led to housing price increases when second-home demand occurs. The primary externalities affecting housing supply are the geographic limitations of the island, and the land-use, zoning, and growth-management regulations that limit housing development. Also the data indicate that Martha's Vineyard has a significant number of second-home owners who have earned their wealth in economies external to Martha's Vineyard and whose demand for the housing on the island has led to increased housing prices. The data indicate that housing is unaffordable to community residents and has become more unaffordable between 1990 and 2000; and local residents are being displaced as existing units are converted to second homes.

Housing Intervention

When market failure occurs, an intervention is necessary to correct the failure. The housing literature identifies the direct public provision of housing and the facilitation or enablement of private housing development by the public or government as the two primary types of interventions that have been successful in addressing market failure.

The literature also identifies the need for a community to decide to intervene when market failure occurs. If the housing market fails and the community does not intervene, the market failure will remain. Only by choosing to act can the community intervene and address the market failure.

Motivation for Intervention

All of the Martha's Vineyard interviewees identified a reaction to community events as the primary reason Martha's Vineyard intervened in the housing market. As mentioned earlier, during the 1990s, housing prices on the island were driven by demand from second-home buyers from economies external to Martha's Vineyard, and housing prices became unaffordable to the island's middle class. The lack of housing for that group of residents became a crisis. Long-time residents were moving off the island, either forced off by the inability to find housing or capitalizing on the island's increased housing prices by selling their homes and moving to the mainland. As community residents left, they were being replaced by second-home owners, who were less active in the community. Residents became concerned that community was being lost and the character of the island destroyed.

> *"Ten years ago it was not a crisis; housing was*
> *still affordable. Now the middle class is getting*
> *shut out. The summer shuffle has led to threats*
> *of loss of community."*

Effect of Intervention

The genesis of Martha's Vineyard's affordable housing interventions is the island's conference in 2000, *Preserving Community: Housing Our Island Families.* Following this conference, Martha's Vineyard created several affordable housing programs, increased the staff of the Dukes County Regional Housing Authority, and reactivated the locally controlled but dormant Island Affordable Housing Fund.

Since the conference, 51 new affordable housing units have been created, a goal of creating 205 new affordable housing units by 2005 has been established, program infrastructure has been created to handle housing problems in the long term, and $1.9 million has been raised from private sources for the island's affordable housing interventions (Island Affordable Housing 2002; Martha's Vineyard Interviews 2002).

According to the 2000 U.S. Census, there were 7,995 second-home units on Martha's Vineyard, almost 54 percent of the housing units on the island. Yet, as of 2001, it was estimated that Martha's Vineyard had only 160 affordable units, including the 51 units created since the 2000 affordable housing conference (Massachusetts Department of Housing 2002; Island Affordable Housing Fund 2002). At 2.33 persons per unit, these affordable units house 373 persons, approximately 2.5 percent of the island's population.

Table 10–3. Housing and population in Martha's Vineyard, Massachusetts

	Number	Percent
Resident housing units		
Affordable housing units	160	1.1
Free-market housing units	6,681	45.0
Total resident housing units	6,841	46.1
Second-home units	7,995	53.9
Total housing units	14,836	100.0
Average persons per units	2.33	
Population		
In affordable units	373	2.5
In free-market units	14,614	97.5
Total population	14,987	100.0

Source: U.S. Census 2000; Massachusetts Department of Housing 2002; Island Affordable Housing Fund 2002 a.

Martha's Vineyard's housing interventions have occurred in the past two years and, as the data indicate, have affected only a small percentage of island residents to date. The goals of the housing intervention programs are modest. Should the community achieve the 2005 goal of 205 new affordable units, based on the average number of persons per unit given in the census, the housing interventions would affect 732 residents, approximately 4.9 percent of the population.

Programs

The housing interventions on Martha's Vineyard include creating awareness of the housing issues among island residents and businesses, articulating a vision for affordable housing on the island, developing an infrastructure to support the creation of that housing, creating multiple programs to provide the housing, and changing land-use and zoning regulations to support affordable housing.

Interviews with the community leaders identified the need for buy-in from the community and local businesses as a critical element in Martha's Vineyard's housing interventions. Permanent island residents and long-term summer residents were cited as having a history of generosity and support for community causes, and a goal of the housing intervention strategy was to present a vision of affordable housing on the island that complemented the existing community, allowing community generosity to be accessed in support of affordable housing development.

> *"We have articulated a vision of affordable hous-*
> *ing that is different. It includes scattered sites,*
> *matches Vineyard style, fits in with the neigh-*
> *borhood. It is not at odds with the neighbor-*
> *hood. We used the model of land conservation.*
> *The summer community supports land conser-*
> *vation. Land conservation and affordable hous-*
> *ing are complementary."*

To achieve its goal of 205 new affordable housing units by 2005, Martha's Vineyard has created four rental housing programs and three ownership programs. The rental programs include (1) a rental subsidy program, modeled after the HUD Section 8 program, in which money that has been donated to the housing fund is used to make up the difference between the free-market rent of a unit and the rent a family is able to pay; (2) a property conversion program, in which the properties are purchased on the free market and converted to affordable rental housing; (3) a revolving loan fund to provide very low interest loans to property owners who convert existing seasonal housing to year-round use as affordable rental housing; and (4) plans for the development of small rental clusters around the island. Ownership programs include (1) down payment assistance in the form of low-interest loans for new home buyers; (2) a "homes on the move" program, in which existing houses that an owner wishes to demolish so a bigger house can be built on the site are instead donated to the housing fund, moved to a new location, and used as affordable housing; and (3) a payment subsidy to developers who build new affordable housing units (Ryan 2001; Martha's Vineyard Interviews 2002; Island Affordable Housing Fund 2002 b). In addition, the Island Affordable Housing Fund has begun to actively solicit the donation of land from island residents, which will be set aside for future affordable housing development. Table 10–4 summarizes the goals of Martha's Vineyard's affordable housing programs.

Table 10–4. Affordable housing programs in Martha's Vineyard

	Expected # of units
Rental programs	
Rental subsidy	40
Purchase of existing units and conversion to affordable rental units	10
Revolving loan fund for conversion of private units to affordable rental units	30
Public development of new rental units	40
Total rental units	120
Ownership programs	
Down payment assistance	20
Houses on the move program	20
Subsidy to developers creating affordable units	45
Total ownership units	85
Total units	205

Source: Island Affordable Housing Fund 2002 a.

The six towns that make up Martha's Vineyard exist as independent political entities, free to set their own zoning and land-use regulations. Interviews with the community leaders indicate that several communities are beginning to adjust zoning laws in an effort to provide affordable housing by allowing the development of undersized or substandard lots, provided the use is restricted to affordable housing; by encouraging the development or conversion of "in-law" apartments to affordable resident housing; and by legalizing the conversion of seasonal cottages to year-round use, provided the units are used for affordable housing.

> *"It [unaffordable housing] has impacted zoning. Some towns have gone to zoning incentives, to satisfy a need. For example, in Tisbury, undersized lots, unbuildable under zoning, are changed so they can be built if the property is used for restricted housing."*

Deed restrictions are the main mechanism Martha's Vineyard uses to keep the designated affordable units out of the free market. Additionally, because Martha's Vineyard has used primarily private funds for the affordable housing programs, income and other guidelines established for its assistance programs are above the levels typically allowed by government programs. For instance, to qualify for rental assistance, a family on Martha's Vineyard might earn up to 140 percent of area median income, or $82,460, rather than being subject to the restriction of 80 percent of area median income found in government programs. According to one respondent, the reason Martha's Vineyard has chosen to rely on private programs to finance its affordable housing activities is a belief that the income limitations of state and federal government programs do not realistically reflect the cost of living on the island, and a belief that those income limitations need to be higher in an island community (Island Affordable Housing Fund 2002 b; Martha's Vineyard Interviews 2002).

Summary

The housing literature cites the need for intervention when market failure occurs, and identifies the direct public provision of housing units and programs that facilitate the private development of housing units as effective intervention strategies. The intervention literature also cites the need for the community to react when a housing crisis occurs and to support the housing intervention politically and financially. Community leaders have recognized the existence of a housing crisis on the island and have reacted with a combination of private and public intervention strategies. The leaders have created public awareness of the housing crisis to develop community, political, and financial support for an intervention, and have devised multiple programs to provide affordable housing. Unique in Martha's Vineyard's strategy is the almost exclusive use of private funding for its affordable housing interventions, notwithstanding the literature that has identified public funds as the primary source of funding for housing programs.

Housing interventions in Martha's Vineyard

- Created awareness of affordable housing issues
- Sought community and political support to address issues
- Instituted multiple programs targeted at affordable housing creation
- Relies almost exclusively on local private funding

Community Concerns

Martha's Vineyard is accessible only by water or by air, making a daily commute from the mainland difficult and expensive. As a result, it is necessary for those who work on Martha's Vineyard to also live there. During interviews, housing and community leaders indicated that unaffordable housing was making it difficult for people to continue to live on the island and was forcing people off the island. The middle class could not afford to purchase houses, and it is very difficult to find affordable year-round rentals. As a result, it has become difficult to attract tourism workers and others, including teachers, medical professionals, and civil servants.

> *"It's impacting the supply of community members, workers, Little League coaches, members for town boards. When the existing people move, they are replaced by seasonal buyers and retirees. You have the negative of losing families and not getting the same back."*

All of the interviewees believed that the continued conversion of island properties to second-home use was having a negative effect on the character of the community. New homes were being constructed that were too large and not in keeping with the character of the island, and existing homes were being expanded without regard for the impact on the neighborhood.

Additionally, interviewees believed that the shortage of housing has affected service levels. The wealthy summer people have high service expectations, but many businesses cannot find enough help during the summer months, which has led to their inability to provide the expected levels of service. There is concern that the worker shortages are hurting the economy and the image of the island.

Finally, two interview respondents expressed concern regarding the cost of living on the island. Whatever is not produced locally must be brought in from the mainland, and transportation costs add to what is-land residents must pay. The interviewees thought the cost of goods on the island was 25 percent higher than on the mainland; this higher cost, combined with lower-than-average incomes and expensive housing, was one reason community members left the island, and it contributed to the difficulty the community faced in attracting workers.

Summary of Research Findings

The research indicates that the housing market on Martha's Vineyard has failed, having been negatively affected by externalities, including second-home demand by buyers from external economies, topographi-cal constraints, and land-use and zoning regulations. The topographical constraints and land-use and zoning regulations have limited the supply of housing, and second-home buyers have increased the demand, which has led to increased housing costs and to a situation in which commu-nity residents cannot afford housing.

Martha's Vineyard has reacted to the housing market failure the way the theoretical model of housing market intervention indicates, by treat-ing it as a community crisis and intervening in the market. The island's intervention strategy includes two elements not specifically addressed in the intervention literature: efforts by community leaders to publicize the housing crisis in an effort to obtain political and community support for implementation of the interventions, and significant program funding from private sources.

Overall, Martha's Vineyard appears to have had initial success with its housing interventions, raising public awareness of housing issues, es-tablishing programs for affordable housing, obtaining partial funding for the implementation of the programs, and developing a limited number of affordable units during the first two years of the program. But the inter-ventions are still in their early stages and have not yet had a significant impact on the island's housing crisis; and community leaders continue to express concern about lost community and difficulty in attracting workers.

11

Provincetown, Massachusetts: A Community at the Crossroads

Provincetown is a summer beach-and-artist community on the northern tip of Cape Cod, approximately 115 surface miles from Boston and 65 miles from the beginning of the cape. The primary access to Provincetown is via Route 6, a two-lane local road running the length of the upper cape from the town of Orleans to Provincetown. According to the 2000 U.S. Census, Provincetown has a year-round population of 3,431. It is governed primarily by a town manager form of government, as well as by Barnstable County.

Provincetown is bounded by water, with the Atlantic Ocean to the north and east, and Cape Cod Bay to the south and west. The land at the end of Cape Cod forms a hook at Provincetown, with a natural harbor on the inside of the hook. The residential and commercial areas of town are located along the harbor on the south side. Route 6 runs along the north side. The northern parts of town lands are beach and dune areas, part of the Cape Cod National Seashore, where development is restricted. The development along the harbor reflects Provincetown's history as a seaport and the unsuitability of the dune areas for development.

Provincetown was the original landing site of the Mayflower in 1620. The Pilgrims spent their first winter in the Provincetown/Truro area before moving on to Plymouth, Massachusetts, the next spring (Schneider 2000; Cunningham 2002). The settlement of Provincetown as a fishing community began in the early 1700s; the town then developed as a point of commerce and safe harbor for fishing and merchant vessels. Fishing remained an important part of the local economy through 1992, when a fishing moratorium was imposed on the Stellwagen Bank area of the Atlantic Ocean, the primary source of fish for Provincetown's fishing industry.

Key events in Provincetown
1620   Pilgrims on the Mayflower arrive in Provincetown
1700s Provincetown becomes fishing town and commercial port
1873   Railroad connecting Provincetown to Boston opens
1899   First art school opens
1918   Artists, writers, and performers summer in Provincetown
1950s Gays adopt Provincetown as summer home
1980s Gay and lesbian community becomes political and economic force
1992   Fishing moratorium imposed on Stellwagen Banks Fishing industry in Provincetown dies

Provincetown's transformation from a fishing village to an artist's colony and resort community began in 1873, when the railroad connecting Boston to Provincetown was completed (Cunningham 2002). The town was officially incorporated in 1893 (Schneider 2000). The first art school was established in 1899. By the end of World War I, the town was home to numerous artists and art schools, attracted by its out-of-the-way location, cheap rents, and sexual tolerance (Cunningham 2002). The gay community began arriving in Provincetown in the 1950s, and by the 1980s were the dominant political and economic force in the community (Manso 2002).

Provincetown Research

Provincetown was identified as a case site through a review of the online archives of the regional newspaper, the *Cape Cod Times,* which contains articles noting that Provincetown had a severe housing crisis (Dooley 2002). The community was selected as the negative case site for this research after a telephone discussion with town officials confirmed that Provincetown did have a housing crisis but had not significantly intervened in the housing market.

Data were collected in Provincetown using a series of guided semi-structured interviews with key informants. Interviewees responded to a series of prepared questions that were designed to probe their knowledge and understanding of the housing and tourism issues affecting the town. Primary data used for this research came from the United States census; secondary data included reports published on the community's Web site, articles published in the Cape Cod Times, and two books that provided a historical perspective on the community.

Tourism

Provincetown is known as a summer resort community, a shopping area, an artist's colony, and a gay and lesbian community. Its numerous beaches and natural areas attract summer visitors. Provincetown is marketed to the gay and lesbian community as a hot spot and "happening place," with many businesses, clubs, and restaurants focused on gay and lesbian customers, an active night life, and a general acceptance of alternative lifestyles by the community. Provincetown's art schools and art galleries are marketed as tourism attractions, and the town's Commercial Street is marketed as a shopping district, with many restaurants and unique shops. It is not uncommon for Provincetown's streets to be filled with busloads of shoppers during the day and with gay and lesbian partiers at night.

Provincetown is a resort community where the rich and famous can congregate without attracting attention.

> *"The community includes Norman Mailer and his wife, George Plimpton, many millionaires, Hollywood and New York theater people, Stanley Kunitz, the poet laureate of the United States. You can sit next to Colin Powell having soup at the Lobster Pot. The celebrities can be in town and not be the center of attention."*

Most tourists arrive in Provincetown via cars, although bus trips are offered from other parts of Massachusetts, ferry service is available to and from Boston, and a small airport offers flights to Boston, New Bedford, and other towns on the cape. The tourism industry serves a mix of day-trippers who come to shop or go to the beach, and extended-stay guests who spend one or more nights. Provincetown has few large hotels. Many smaller guest houses or bed-and-breakfasts offer the bulk of overnight accommodations.

Tourism is an important part of Provincetown's economy. Most of the town's businesses are directly or indirectly related to tourism. Compared to Massachusetts and the United States as a whole, more than twice as many of the town's businesses are retail and almost four times as many are directly related to tourism. Table 11–1 presents Provincetown's business establishments by industry.

The interview respondents confirmed the importance of tourism to Provincetown's economy. Besides the tourism businesses, the only other employers of significance identified in the community are the town itself and a town-owned nursing home. One of the community leaders indicated that even those local residents who hold other jobs often work part-time in tourism.

> *"Most people are shopkeepers, waiters, bartenders, food vendors. Some people pick up part-time work in tourism."*

Provincetown actively markets itself as an artists' enclave, as a tourism destination to the gay and lesbian community, and as a destination for tourists seeking a summer beach community. The town has imposed a room revenue tax that is used to market the community; the tax has also been used to enhance the community for tourists and residents through increased public services, such as an additional trash pickup at night to keep the town clean, and for public improvements aimed at tourists, such as new public restrooms and new benches throughout the town.

The tourism workers in Provincetown include members of the new immigrant, seeker, locals, and managerial groups identified by Adler and Adler (1999). (See chapter 7 for a full description of the groups.) Summer workers who are members of the new immigrant group include Jamaicans and students from the Czech Republic. The seeker group includes U.S. college students who spend the summer at the beach, and gays and lesbians who have moved to Provincetown to experience the lifestyle. Most

Table 11–1. Business establishments by industry in Provincetown, Massachusetts, and the United States (percent)

	Provincetown	Massachusetts	United States
Tourism establishments			
Arts, entertainment & recreation	1.7	1.5	1.5
Accommodation & food services	32.9	8.3	7.7
Total tourism establishments	34.5	9.8	9.1
Other establishments			
Construction	3.5	9.3	10.0
Real estate & rental & leasing	3.8	3.4	4.2
Retail trade	32.2	14.6	15.8
Finance & insurance	1.4	5.1	6.0
Professional, scientific & technical	3.3	12.0	10.2
Other	21.3	45.9	44.6
Total other establishments	65.5	90.2	90.9
Total establishments	100.0	100.0	100.0

Source: 2000 County Business Patterns, U.S. Census Bureau; Provincetown business establishment data.

of the town's businesses are locally owned, with the local and managerial groups consisting of many of the same people.

Housing Market Failure Analysis

As discussed more fully in Part 2, Theoretical Foundations, according to housing market theory, market failure occurs when negative externalities exist that alter the efficient functioning of the market and lead to the increase of housing costs beyond the means of local residents. The literature identifies three primary types of externalities that affect housing in tourism communities: second-home demand; growth-management, land-use, and zoning regulations; and topographical constraints. The literature also identifies the elasticity of market demand—the ability or inability of those seeking housing to shift to another community—as a key factor affecting housing prices.

If these externalities are present in Provincetown, the conditions for market failure exist, and high housing costs and displaced local residents can be expected.

Housing Market

The data indicate that housing is unaffordable to local residents in Provincetown. Table 11–2 presents housing affordability data. The median household income is 35 percent lower in Provincetown than in Massachusetts, and 22 percent lower than in the United States. Census data also show that as of 2000, the median house price was 74 percent higher in Provincetown than in Massachusetts, and 172 percent higher than in the United States. The ratio of house prices to household income shown in table 11–2 allows the comparison of relative housing affordability across different housing markets. These ratios show that as of 2000, relative housing costs in Provincetown were more than twice those in Massachusetts and more than three times those in the United States. Additionally, the data indicate that this ratio increased by 39 percent between 1990 and 2000 for Provincetown, indicating that housing was 39 percent less affordable in 2000 than it was in 1990 (U. S. Census 1990 and 2000).

Table 11–2 also presents a comparison of the money a median-income family has available for housing expenses monthly, assuming the family

Table 11–2. Housing affordability in Provincetown, Massachusetts, and the United States

	Provincetown		Massachusetts		United States	
	2000	1990	2000	1990	2000	1990
Housing units that are second homes	47.0%	37.2%	3.6%	3.7%	3.1%	3.0%
Median household income	$32,716	$20,847	$50,502	$36,952	$41,994	$30,056
Median house price	$323,600	$148,100	$185,700	$162,000	$119,000	$79,100
Ratio of house price to household income	9.9	7.1	3.7	4.4	2.8	2.6
Available funds monthly for housing at 30% of median household income	$818	$521	$1,263	$924	$1,050	$751
Monthly cost for median-priced house	$1,940	$888	$1,113	$971	$713	$474
Excess income or (income gap)	($1,122)	($367)	$149	($47)	$336	$277
Households paying more than 30% of income for housing	40.7%	49.1%	27.8%	31.0%	26.9%	27.3%

Source: 1990 and 2000 United States Census.

spends a maximum of 30 percent of income for housing and purchases a median-priced house using a 6 percent, 30-year mortgage. As of 2000, median-income families in Massachusetts and the United States could afford to purchase a median-priced house, but median-income families in Provincetown could not; their incomes would have to increase by 137 percent in order to effect a purchase.

The data also show that more than 40 percent of the households in Provincetown pay more than 30 percent of their income for housing, 46 percent more than in the rest of Massachusetts and 51 percent more than in the United States overall.

The interviews confirmed that housing is very expensive in Provincetown. One community leader indicated that as of 2002, housing prices had risen to an average of $399,000, making Provincetown the community with the second highest housing prices in Massachusetts, trailing only Nantucket.

Interview respondents identified several factors believed to affect housing prices in Provincetown. They all indicated that housing is being purchased by people from out of town and converted to second homes. The second homes are being purchased by wealthy people who do not need to rent their units to pay the mortgage. This has resulted in the removal from the market of rentals that were formerly available to tourism workers and local residents.

> *"There is no more affordable housing. There is no more rental housing. They have become second homes. They leave them empty most of the time. This is versus the locals who needed the income from the rentals. This displaces the locals and artists. These people want housing."*

This was confirmed by town data, which indicated that between 1997 and 2000, the number of year-round housing units declined by 323, more than 13.5 percent of the town's resident housing stock (Town of Provincetown 2002).

Two interviewees indicated that Provincetown is losing resident housing as larger houses are purchased, converted to guest houses, and then used as lodging for tourists. Many of the guest houses make basement and other smaller rooms available as housing for employees; however, overall, the guest-house conversions are thought to reduce the number of resident units available.

Growth-management and zoning regulations were also identified by two of the interview respondents as factors affecting housing prices. Provincetown's growth-management regulations limit the amount of development that may take place, allowing only 17 new residential units per year. The community's zoning regulations limit the height of new buildings to a maximum of two stories and restrict changes in the appearance of buildings throughout the town (Cunningham 2002; Provincetown Interviews 2002).

Topographic limitations in Provincetown include the beach and dune areas that surround the town center. Historically this land had not been developed because it could not support housing or commercial activities; more recently the land has been designated national seashore, which prevents any future development. Overall, the only land in Provincetown that can be developed is that where the existing town sits, and any future development needs to be done within the confines of this space (Cunningham 2002: Provincetown Interviews 2002).

Summary

The data indicate that housing in Provincetown has been negatively affected by externalities, including second-home demand, topographical constraints, and zoning and growth-management regulations. The data also show that housing is unaffordable to community residents and that local residents are being displaced. Provincetown has experienced a housing market failure.

Housing Intervention

When market failure occurs, an intervention is necessary to correct it. The literature identifies the direct public provision of housing and the public enablement of private housing development as the two primary successful methods of housing intervention.

When a housing market failure occurs in a community, a housing crisis also occurs, and it is followed by complaints from local residents about housing costs. At the crisis stage, the community faces two choices: to act or not to act. If the community chooses not to act, an intervention does not occur, and market failure persists. If the community chooses to act, a housing intervention is the next step. Once it has been determined that market failure has occurred, the most critical decision a community must make is whether to act or not.

Motivation for Intervention

Provincetown was selected as the nonintervention case site for this research because preliminary information indicated that interventions had not occurred. From a research perspective, it was critical to determine if Provincetown had or had not intervened in the housing market, and if it had intervened, what the motivation for intervention was.

The interview data and secondary data indicate that Provincetown intervened in the housing market initially not in reaction to market failure conditions but in response to Massachusetts state regulations.

I found that Provincetown's primary motivation for intervention was the 1997 Massachusetts Housing Partnership Act, which requires all communities in the state to have 10 percent of their housing stock designated as affordable. Affordable housing units under the Housing Partnership Act include units not only for working individuals and families but also for seniors, people with disabilities, and people with HIV (Massachusetts Department of Housing and Community Development 2002; Provincetown Interviews 2002; Town of Provincetown 2002).

> *"The big motivation was the 1997 Housing Partnership Act. This was a pioneer for the state."*

In addition, Provincetown has begun to perceive a developing community housing crisis and has begun to assess the need for affordable housing beyond the state mandates.

> *"In 2001, we had a housing awareness campaign. We studied town employees. Who lives in town? How many committees had vacancies? Try to remember those who left."*

Although Provincetown has begun to consider the existence of a housing crisis in the community and has begun to consider interventions specifically in response to that crisis, the interventions had not been implemented at the time of this research.

Effect of Intervention

According to the 2000 United States census, 47 percent of the housing units in Provincetown were second homes and 53 percent were occupied by community residents. Of the 2,062 housing units occupied by community residents, only 135 were affordable or subsidized housing units designated for use by families, seniors, and others. These units housed approximately 228 persons, 6.6 percent of the town's population (Massachusetts Department of Housing 2002; U.S. Census 2000). Table 11–3 summarizes Provincetown's housing and population.

Table 11–3. Housing and population in Provincetown

	Number	Percent
Resident housing units		
Affordable housing units	135	3.5
Free-market housing units	1,927	49.5
Total resident housing units	2,062	53.0
Second-home units	1,828	47.0
Total housing units	3,890	100.0
Average persons per units	1.69	
Population in affordable units	228	6.6
Population in free-market units	3,203	93.4
Total population	3,431	100.0

Source: U.S. Census 2000; Massachusetts Department of Housing and Community Development.

The town's public efforts to provide affordable and subsidized housing have been limited and have focused on a mix of housing units. Of the 61 units owned and managed by the Provincetown Housing Authority, only 9 were designated for use by families. The remaining 52 public units include 24 for senior housing, 18 for persons with disabilities, and 10 for persons with HIV (Town of Provincetown 1999). Private developers have provided the remaining 74 affordable housing units in Provincetown.

Two interview respondents expressed concern that the privately developed affordable housing units were priced beyond the reach of working families in the community, and that the programs were failing to have the desired impact on the community.

Programs

Provincetown has used public programs and public funds to create affordable housing units, and has created incentives for their development by private entities. As mentioned earlier, in 1980, the community enacted growth-management regulations that significantly limit the number of housing units that can be constructed each year. A recent modification to the regulations granted a priority in the permitting process to developers who include affordable housing units in their developments.

> *"We give priority to building communities with affordable housing in them. We issue 17 bedroom permits per year. There is a three-year lead time to get a permit. But if you make at least 25 percent of the units affordable, you get to the top of the list."*

Additional affordable housing was created in Provincetown through the reallocation of unused bedroom permits. The town identified 91 bedroom units (approximately 53 housing units) that had been allocated since the institution of growth management in 1980 but had not been built, and reallocated all those permits to affordable housing, as an incentive for private development.

Funding for Provincetown's public affordable housing programs has come from federal and state housing agencies such as HUD or the Massachusetts Department of Housing and Community Development. Funds have been used for the development of affordable housing and for the conversion of existing units into affordable housing. Affordable housing developed in Provincetown is kept affordable through the use of deed restrictions, some of which are permanent and some of which expire after a set period.

In addition to the existing affordable housing programs, Provincetown's affordable housing strategy includes the prospective use of two new programs. The community has proposed the creation of a housing trust fund for the development of affordable housing and is seeking approval from the Massachusetts state legislature to impose a tax on real estate transfers that would be paid to that fund. Also, a controversial affordable housing program has been proposed that would provide a 100 percent property tax exemption to the owners of apartments who convert the units to affordable housing.

Summary

Affordable housing units have been developed in Provincetown by the local government and by private developers who have reacted to incentives established by the local government. The public development and enablement of affordable housing units is consistent with the types of interventions identified in the literature.

Provincetown's housing interventions
• **Development, with direct construction of affordable housing units** • **Enablement, with regulations that include incentives for affordable housing units** • **Real estate transfer tax dedicated to affordable housing development (proposed)** • **Property tax exemption for the creation of affordable units (proposed)**

Provincetown's primary motivation for housing interventions, however, is not consistent with the literature. The literature identifies community reaction to a housing market failure as the motivation for interventions, but Provincetown's primary motivation has been compliance with state regulations. Although the need for housing interventions has become a topic of debate in the community, Provincetown had not yet chosen to intervene in reaction to a market failure as of 2002.

Community Concerns

Two interview respondents expressed concern that much of the affordable housing developed in Provincetown was priced too high and was not affordable to the residents most in need. This concern was particularly focused on the privately developed affordable housing units, which were believed to be beyond the means of most town residents. Additionally, interviewees were concerned that the affordable housing efforts were not being directed at the seasonal workers, who were most in need and often lived in overcrowded or substandard conditions in old buildings in the community or in neighboring towns.

Two interview respondents expressed concern that Provincetown was losing its community and its sense of place as tourism continues to develop, the fishing industry dies, and long-time residents move away. As stated earlier, the fishing economy began to collapse in 1992 when a fishing moratorium was imposed; since then the fishermen and their families have been selling their properties and moving elsewhere. They have been replaced by second-home owners, a significant portion of whom are members of the gay and lesbian community who use their properties only part of the year and whose values regarding the community differ from the departing residents.

> *"Community leaves as the houses turn over. The replacement buyers are not members of the community. They are not on committees and boards. There is no neighbor to turn to. The out-of-town buyer receives the benefits of the arts and conservation, but they are not active in creating these."*

Additionally, interview respondents identified increased property assessments and taxes as a growing concern. The assessments rise as property values rise and taxes are increased to pay for community services such as schools, which are used by fewer and fewer residents. The regional high school in Provincetown is an important part of the community's identity; yet only one baby was born in Provincetown in 2000, and the number of families with children is declining.

> *"No young families with children are moving in. It's unaffordable. There are not social activities for families with kids. We spend $80,000 per kid to educate."*

Another concern expressed by one interview respondent was that some of the proposed affordable housing solutions—particularly a property tax abatement for converting apartments to affordable housing—would cause a further increase in taxes and would hurt local residents and small business owners.

One interview respondent was concerned because the room revenue tax was being spent solely on infrastructure when it could also be used to offset some of the negative costs tourism development imposed on local residents, such as a housing affordability crisis.

Finally, one interview respondent indicated that the cost of housing was driving Provincetown's artists away, which could ultimately affect the community's tourism. The artists have discussed leaving Provincetown en masse and relocating to another community where housing is more affordable.

> *"There is an active movement in the artist community to leave as a group. They are looking for creative soul. They are looking for communities to move to that offer the spirit of creativity, and where they can afford housing."*

Summary of Research Findings

The research data indicate that a housing market failure has occurred in Provincetown. Growth-management regulations, zoning regulations, topographical constraints, and second-home demand have been identified as externalities affecting the community, which have led to increased housing prices and displaced local residents.

Affordable housing units in Provincetown have been developed using public programs and public funds, and have been developed privately in reaction to development incentives. Provincetown's motivation for the creation of the existing housing programs differs from the theory, which states that interventions occur in reaction to market failure and a community crisis. The primary reason identified for Provincetown's housing interventions was a state mandate that communities create affordable housing.

Overall, the research data indicate mixed results for Provincetown's housing programs. Affordable housing units have been created, but housing remains very unaffordable in the community, and two-thirds of the interview respondents believe the existing interventions have been ineffective because the units created are priced too high and are not targeted at the core of the community. The community was discussing other housing interventions at the time this research was conducted, but none had yet been implemented.

Appendix:
Research Method and Data Collection

An in-depth study of four tourism communities was conducted using the case study research method. Specifically, the research is an explanatory case study, presented using a multiple-case-study structure. Qualitative data were gathered using guided semi-structured interviews, with additional data from primary and secondary sources; the data were analyzed using the explanation building analysis technique.

The Case Study Research Method

As with any research, alternative methods might have been chosen. The case study technique was selected as the method for this research because of the questions and events to be examined. Several key elements point to the case study research method as being appropriate for this research. First, according to the noted sociological researcher Robert Yin, the case study is the preferred research method when "how" and "why" questions are posed. This research asks why a housing imbalance exists, why the communities have intervened in the housing market, and how they have intervened. The research focuses on the housing situation in the communities; the programs, policies, and other processes the communities used to intervene in the market (the "how"); the motivation for the communities to intervene in the market (the "why"); and the effect of the intervention on the communities (the "what" and the "lessons learned").

Second, this research deals with contemporary events. The housing market interventions in the selected case study communities had occurred and were occurring at the time of the research, and therefore the events could be studied in real time, using qualitative data obtained from community leaders and others active in the intervention. The case study research method is appropriate for investigating contemporary phenomena within a real-life context and when the events are more contemporary than historical (Yin 1994).

Third, this research focused on events over which I had no control. The housing interventions occurred independently from this research, and would continue to occur or not occur in tourism communities in the absence of this research. When the investigator has little or no control over the events, the case study is an appropriate research method (Yin 1994).

Finally, the research focused on events that occur in a community. The case study does not need to focus on an individual or enterprise but can focus on any collection or population of interest (Stake 1978). According to Berg (2001), the case study research method should be used when the investigator needs to develop an understanding of the events occurring in a community.

A case study may include one or more cases; a multiple-case study involves two or more cases. According to Yin (1994), a multiple-case study offers the researcher the opportunity to develop a general explanation of events from an analysis of the common elements in the individual cases. Multiple-case-study research offers the opportunity for replication of results in the same way that multiple experiments can lead to replication of results. The evidence from multiple-case studies is often regarded as more compelling than the evidence from a single case study. If similar results are obtained in multiple cases in which the same research method is used, than replication is said to have taken place (Yin 1994). The multiple-case-study structure has been used in this research to gather evidence from multiple communities that may be analyzed for replication. The analysis of this evidence (as discussed below) will determine whether replication has taken place.

The two main types of case study research are the exploratory case study and the explanatory case study. An exploratory or descriptive case study describes relationships or events. In contrast, an explanatory case study explains observed events in the context of theories. The goal in a multiple-case explanatory case study is to develop a general explanation that fits each of the individual cases, even though the case details differ, and to explain causal links in complex interventions (Yin 1994). I used the explanatory case study method for this research.

Case study results can be generalized in much the same way the results of an experiment can be generalized, when multiple sources of data have been used and triangulated, multiple cases have been studied (multiple experiments), and data have been analyzed with rigor. The generalizations that can derive from case study research are described as analytic generalizations; the results can be generalized to theories. Because of their nature, case study results cannot be statistically generalized (Yin 1994). Analytic generalization of the case results were made in this research.

Case Site Selection
A key element in the design of case study research is the selection of the case sites. It is important that case sites be selected using established criteria. An initial step in this research was the establishment of criteria for the sites to be studied. The criteria established were:
- The community had to be an established tourism community.
- Tourism had to be a key part of the community's economy.
- The community had to be geographically or otherwise discrete.
- There must have been a community intervention in the housing market.

The first two criteria are the most important. The communities selected for study needed to be generally recognized as tourist destinations, with established tourist-related businesses, including attractions, hotels and other overnight accommodations, and restaurants; and tourism needed to be a key part of the community's economy as indicated by quantifiable indicators, such as a percentage of tourism employees in excess of the state and national averages or a percentage of second homes significantly in excess of the state and national averages. Additionally, the community needed to be geographically or otherwise discrete so that it could be analyzed without extensive overlap from other communities and from other nontourism influences outside the community.

Finally, because the research questions focus on the how and why of community intervention in the housing market, an intervention by the community (its government, government agencies, for-profit or nonprofit agencies, or its citizens) must have taken place in the housing market in the sites chosen for study. Communities where for-profit tourism businesses react to market forces and provide housing for their employees but where the community has not intervened were not considered because this is an element of efficient market functioning rather than market failure. Additionally, housing markets in centrally planned tourism destinations were considered only to the extent that there continued to be active government intervention. Communities where the only government role has been planning, without ongoing intervention, were excluded.

Of the four case sites selected for this research, the preliminary evidence for three indicated there had been a community intervention in the housing market (the positive case sites); the fourth site met all the other criteria, but the preliminary evidence indicated there had not been a community intervention in the housing market (the negative case site). The inclusion of a negative case site allowed for a comparison of motivation between communities that intervened and communities that did not intervene.

The three positive case sites are Martha's Vineyard, Massachusetts; Aspen, Colorado; and Whistler, British Columbia, Canada; the negative case site is Provincetown, Massachusetts.

As described more fully in the chapters on the individual communities, the sites meet the selection criteria established. All four sites are established tourism communities where tourism is an important part of the local economy. Each site has a discrete housing market, without much overlap into surrounding communities; the three positive case sites appeared to have an ongoing community intervention in the housing market, where the why, how, and what research questions could be asked, and where the market failure hypothesis could be tested; and the negative case site appeared not to have active intervention in the housing market.

In addition to meeting the criteria established for selection, the sites chosen offered several other benefits. The initial interventions in the Aspen and Whistler housing markets occurred more than ten years ago, so it has been possible to study the effects of the interventions over time. Also, because Whistler is outside of the United States, it provides a different perspective on housing intervention. Finally, each of the three positive case sites has intervened in the housing market in a different way, so it has been possible to identify more than one effective housing intervention strategy.

Data Techniques

Triangulation is the use of multiple sources of data from multiple data-gathering techniques to investigate the same phenomenon. The triangulation of data in case study research is critical to the development of an analytic generalization. The use of multiple data sources strengthens the case study, assists with the ability to generalize the results, and allows more convincing and accurate conclusions to be reached. The typical sources of evidence to verify facts in case study research include open-end interviews, documents, and archival records (Yin 1994). For this research I used interview data, primary records, and secondary data, consisting of local documents and publications.

The purpose of the interview in a case study is to obtain not only the facts but also the respondent's opinions about the events (Yin 1994, 84). The interview can be used to obtain descriptions of events, explanations, and linkages to prior and subsequent events (Stake 1995, 65). I used interviews in this research to obtain the opinions of the interviewees regarding how the community acted to address housing issues, why the community took these actions, and what effect the actions had on the community.

I conducted guided semi-structured interviews with key informants in the case site communities. In a guided semi-structured interview, the researcher uses a series of prepared questions, asked in a systematic and consistent order, to delve into the knowledge of the respondent; however, the interviewer is free to digress from the prepared questions in order to probe more deeply into specific issues that may not be known beforehand.

As a guide for the interviews, I prepared questions in eight primary categories:

- community characteristics
- tourism
- housing
- trends affecting the community
- programs
- costs
- program effects
- lessons learned

Each category contained multiple questions that could be asked until a full response was obtained. For instance, to identify the tourism trends affecting the community, one question asked respondents to name "tourism-related things that have been affecting the community." Subsequent questions in this category asked respondents to identify positive things or benefits generated from tourism, and to identify issues or problems generated by tourism. These subsequent questions were designed to be asked in the event the initial question did not elicit an encompassing response or did not elicit both positive and negative responses. These questions were also designed to be omitted in the event they had already been answered.

Primary and secondary data about the case site communities were also collected and reviewed. Primary data consist of public records that have been collected and "prepared for the expressed purpose of examination by others" (Berg 2001, 191). Primary data include census and other demographic data, and items such as maps, charts, and community photographs. Secondary data are those originally created or published for another purpose. In this research, secondary data consisted of published documents such as community master plans, strategic plans and reports, and housing plans and reports; and housing authority and planning department operating documents, procedures, and guidelines. Secondary data also include information on the case site published in newspapers, periodicals, or books, and on the Web sites of communities, newspapers, and periodicals.

Data Analysis

Following the completion of the interviews, the data were coded using the data coding techniques of Anselm Strauss and Juliet Corbin (1998) and then analyzed using the explanation building technique (Yin 1994). Data coding involves a line-by-line, or incident-by-incident analysis of the data, in which the researcher classifies the data by similarity or difference, generates categories of data, and discovers relationships and concepts in the data. The data from this research were coded using open coding, axial coding, and selective coding techniques. In open coding, the data were analyzed line-by-line, concepts were identified, and these concepts were refined into categories representing a significant problem, issue, or event that is present in the data. Following the open coding, axial coding was used to develop subcategories from the data and link the subcategories to the categories. The subcategories were then studied to explain the events observed and to seek answers for the where, why, how, who, and what questions. Finally, selective coding was used to integrate and refine categories, relate the categories to theory, and explain what the researcher has observed within the context of theory.

Explanation building is a common technique for the analysis of case study data; the details of the individual cases are examined to build a general explanation that fits all cases. The goal is to build an explanation, or causal links, about the case through the analysis of the data about it (Yin 1994). Explanation building is an iterative technique. First, an initial theoretical statement or proposition about policy is made. The findings of the initial case are then compared against this statement or proposition. Depending on the results of the comparison, the statement or proposition is revised. Other details of the case are then compared against the revised statement or proposition. The process is repeated within the initial case, and within the additional cases in a multiple-case study, until a common explanation is developed. The explanation building technique relies on the researcher's developing a series of initial propositions regarding the events observed or expected to be observed during the case study research, and then continually revising these propositions as the case study data are analyzed.

I followed this explanation building process in this research. I created a series of initial propositions and continually compared them as I coded, categorized, and analyzed the data. In some cases the initial propositions proved correct, such as the initial proposition that the case site community had no primary business other than tourism. Many other initial propositions were continually revised as the data were analyzed. For example, the initial proposition that the housing crisis in the community was caused by an influx of too many workers to support and service the tourists was revised to reflect the finding that one of the major causes of the crisis was increased second-home demand, which removed existing housing from the system.

Once explanations had been built for each individual case, the same process was used to build a general explanation that fit all the cases. The analytical generalizations of this research are presented in chapter 1.

Glossary

affordable housing. Requires no more than 30 percent of a household's income. Other definitions—that refer to measurements of housing expenditure per unit of housing services or measurements of income and the ability to spend on housing services versus other basic needs—are not considered in this book.

community. As used in this work, a group of people living in a single geographic area, with a common political, legal, and social structure.

deed. A conveyance instrument given to pass title fee title to a property upon sale (Talamo 1986, 46).

deed restriction. A legally enforceable limitation or restriction on the use of a property that is recorded in the land records of a community and binds current and future owners of the property (Talamo 1986, 46). In the case of affordable housing units, deed restrictions may limit the use of the units to those individuals or families who meet certain eligibility criteria.

externality. A cost or benefit that is external to the market price mechanism.

externalities in tourism communities. Government-imposed regulations, second-home buyers from outside economies, and topographical constraints. Externalities in tourism communities consist of housing regulations, such as land-use and zoning regulations, building codes, environmental regulations, visual-impact regulations, and growth-limiting regulations; the physical and geographic constraints of the land, such as mountains and oceans; and external sources of competition, such as second-home demand. These externalities have an impact on the functioning of the market.

housing crisis. When community residents are displaced from their homes because of increased housing costs relative to income, and when those seeking affordable housing in a community are unable to find it there. A community crisis, which can follow a housing crisis, is indicated by a lack of local residents available to participate on community boards and in volunteer activities, and when the community is unable to attract and retain employees for key industries in the community, such as tourism, or for key community positions, such as in health care, police and fire protection, and education.

housing unit. "A house, an apartment, a mobile home, a group of rooms, or a single room that is occupied (or if vacant, is intended for occupancy) as separate living quarters" (U.S. Census Bureau 2000 a). Collectively, the housing units in a community form the housing stock (or housing) of the community.

second home. A housing unit for seasonal, recreational, or occasional use. Included as second homes are vacant units intended for use on weekends, occasionally throughout the year, only during certain seasons, or as interval ownership properties such as time-share condominiums (U.S. Census Bureau 2000 b). Second homes are not used as primary or permanent residences.

tourism. The travel of nonresidents (tourists) to destination areas, as long as the trip does not result in a new permanent residence, and including travel for both recreational and business purposes. Tourists may be visitors who make at least one overnight stop and stay at least twenty-four hours, and so-called excursionists or day-trippers, who stay less than twenty-four hours and do not make an overnight stop. This definition encompasses the daily tourist, the short-stay tourist, the longer-stay tourist, and those who own second homes in a community. Extended-stay tourists stay at least twenty-four hours and may be second-home owners (Murphy 1985).

tourism community. A community in which tourism occurs and in which tourism businesses and tourism employment occur at rates greater than the national, state, or province rates. In a tourism community, businesses may exist fully or in part to service the needs of tourists. These tourism businesses may include attractions, restaurants, lodging establishments, and tourist-oriented retail businesses; they may also include support businesses such as construction, service businesses, and the government and government agencies.

References

Adler, Patricia A. 1999. Transience and the Postmodern Self: The Geographic Mobility of Resort Workers. *Sociological Quarterly* 40, no. 1, Winter: 31–59.

Adler, Patricia A., and Peter Adler. 1999. Resort Workers: Adaptation in the Leisure-Work Nexus. *Sociological Perspectives* 42, no. 3, Fall: 369–402.

Aspen City Government. 2002. http://www.aspenalive.com/apps/pbcs.dll/article?Site=AA&Date=20020911&Category=CGOV&ArtNo=209110009&Ref=AR&SectionCat=COMMUNITY (accessed 15/08/2002) (site now discontinued).

Aspen (CO) Daily News. 2002. www.aspendailynews.com (accessed 13/05/2002).

Aspen Interviews. 2002. By the author. September 2002.

Aspen (CO) Times. 2002. http://www.aspentimes.com (accessed 13/05/2002).

Barlow-Perez, Sally. 2000. *A History of Aspen.* Basalt, Colorado: WHO Press.

Barnett, Bob. 2000. A Vision for a Valley. In *Whistler: History in the Making,* 12–18. Whistler, British Columbia, Canada: Pique Publications, Inc.

Bator, Francis M. 1958. The Anatomy of Market Failure. *Quarterly Journal of Economics* 72 (3): 351–79. Reprinted in *The Theory of Market Failure: A Critical Examination,* edited by Tyler Cowen, 35–66. Fairfax, VA: George Mason University Press, 1988.

Belcher, John R., and Deborah Rejent. 1993. Using Company-Owned Housing and Workfare to Fill the Need for Low-Wage Workers: A Solution or Step Backward? *Social Work* 38, no. 3: 297–305.

Berg, Bruce L. 2001. *Qualitative Research Methods for the Social Sciences.* Boston: Allyn and Bacon.

Bollom, Chris. 1978. *Attitudes and Second Homes in Rural Wales.* Cardiff, Wales: University of Wales Press.

Bosselman, Fred P., Craig A. Peterson, and Claire McCarthy. 1999. *Managing Tourism Growth: Issues and Applications.* Washington, DC: Island Press.

Bourne, Larry S. 1981. *The Geography of Housing.* London: Edward Arnold (Publishers) Ltd.

Buchanan, James M., and W. C. Stubblebine. 1962. Externality. *Economica* 29: 371–84.

Burke, David. 2002. Survey highlights ongoing need. *Whistler Question* (Whistler, British Columbia, Canada), March 21, www.whistlerquestion.com.

Burns, L. S., R. C. Healy, D. M. McAllister, and B. K. Tjioa. 1977. *The Housing of Nations: Analysis and Policy in a Comparative Framework,* Report for the Agency for International Development. Washington, DC: U.S. Department of State.

Butler, R. W. 1980. The Concept of a Tourist Area Cycle of Evolution: Implication for Management of Resources. *Canadian Geographer* XXIV, no. 1: 5–12.

Cape Cod (MA) Times. 2002. http://www.capecodeonline.com (accessed 13/05/2002).

Carpineto, Jane. 1998. *On the Vineyard.* New York: St. Martin's Press.

Carroll, Rick. 2002, April 21. High-end Aspen homes bouncing back. *Aspen Daily News* http://www.aspendailynews.com/Search_Articels/view_article.cfm?OrderNumber=3968 (accessed 13/05/2002).

City of Aspen. 2000. *2000 Aspen Area Community Plan Update.* Colorado: The City of Aspen.

———. 2002. http://www.aspengov.com/CDComPro/Housing.htm (accessed 13/05/2002).

Coase, R. H. 1960. The Problem of Social Cost. *Journal of Law and Economics* 3 (October): 1–44.

Commonwealth of Massachusetts. 2002. Commonwealth Communities. http://www.state.ma.us/cc/ (accessed 30/04/2002).

Cowan, Tyler, ed. 1988. *The Theory of Market Failure: A Critical Examination.* Fairfax, Virginia: George Mason University Press.

Crawford, Margaret. 1995. *Building the Workingman's Paradise: The Design of American Company Towns.* London: Verso.

Crosby, Rick. 2000. Industrial Evolution. In *Whistler: History in the Making,* 78–83. Whistler, British Columbia, Canada: Pique Publications, Inc.

Cubie, Robyn. 2000. The Nuts and Bolts of Building the Village. In *Whistler: History in the Making*, 90–93. Whistler, British Columbia, Canada: Pique Publications, Inc.

Cunningham, Michael. 2002. *Land's End*. New York: Crown Publishers.

Doogan, Kevin. 1996. *Labour Mobility and the Changing Housing Market. Urban Studies* 33, no. 2: 199–222.

Dooley, Emily C. 2002. Provincetown looks to a new plan for preservation. *Cape Cod (MA) Times*, March 1, 2002. http://capecodonline.com/.

Dukes County Regional Housing Authority. 2000. "Preserving Community: Housing Our Island Families: A forum for Island leaders and people committed to solving the Vineyard's affordable housing crisis," a conference held at Vineyard Haven, Massachusetts.

Economic & Planning Systems, Inc. 2002. *Aspen Affordable Housing Strategic Plan.* Denver, Colorado: Economic & Planning Systems, Inc.

Ferlauto, R. C. 1991. A New Approach to Low-Income Housing: Cooperation Between Unions and Business Is Producing Housing Benefits for Workers. *Public Welfare* 49, no. 3: 30–34.

Gallent, Nick. 1997. Improvement Grants, Second Homes and Planning Control in England and Wales: A Policy Review. *Planning Practice & Research* 12, no. 4, November: 401–11.

Gallent, Nick, and Mark Tewdwr-Jones. 2000. *Rural Second Homes in Europe: Examining housing supply and planning control.* Aldershot, Hampshire, England: Ashgate Publishing Limited.

_____. 2001. Second Homes and the UK Planning System. *Planning Practice & Research* 16, no. 1: 59–69.

Hamel, Jacques, Stephane Dufour, and Dominic Fortin. 1993. *Case Study Methods.* Newbury Park, California: Sage Publications.

Hanushek, Eric A., and John M. Quigley. 1990. Commercial Land Use Regulation and Local Government Finance. *The American Economic Review* 80, no. 2, May: 176–80.

Island Affordable Housing Fund. 2002 a. http://vho.vineyard.net/iahf.html (accessed 24/04/2003) (site now discontinued).

_____. 2002 b. *Raising the Roof.* Vineyard Haven, Massachusetts: The Island Affordable Housing Fund.

Katz, Lawrence, and Kenneth T. Rosen. 1987. The Interjurisdictional Effects of Growth Controls on Housing Prices. *Journal of Law & Economics* 30 (April): 149–60.

Keynes, John Maynard. 1936. *The General Theory of Employment, Interest, and Money.* Reprint, Amherst, New York: Prometheus Books, 1997.

Malpezzi, Stephen. 1996. Housing Prices, Externalities, and Regulation in U.S. Metropolitan Areas. *Journal of Housing Research* 7, no. 2: 209–41.

Malpezzi, Stephen, and Richard J. Green. 1996. What Has Happened to the Bottom of the US Housing Market? *Urban Studies* 33, no. 10: 1807–20.

Manso, Peter. 2002. *Ptown: Art, Sex, and Money on the Outer Cape.* New York: A Lisa Drew Book/Scribner.

Martha's Vineyard Gazette. 2002. http://www.mvgazette.com/ (accessed 26/12/2002).

Martha's Vineyard Interviews. 2002. By the author. July–August 2002.

Martha's Vineyard Times. 2002. http://www.mvtimes.com/ (accessed 26/12/2002).

Massachusetts Department of Housing and Community Development. 2002. Provincetown Community Profile. http://www.state.ma.us.

Massachusetts Department of Housing and Community Development: Subsidized Housing Inventory. 2002. http://www.state.ma.us/dhcd/components/hac/subhous.htm (accessed 09/03/2003).

Maxwell, G. D. 2000. *Buying the Farm. In Whistler: History in the Making,* 100–08. Whistler, British Columbia, Canada: Pique Publications, Inc.

Mills, Frank J. 1995. The Cost of Housing in a Tourist Economy: The US Virgin Islands. In *Environment and Development in the Caribbean: Geographical Perspectives,* edited by David Barker and Duncan F. M. McGregor, 90–107. Kingston, Jamaica: The Press, University of the West Indies.

Murphy, P.E. 1985. *Tourism: A Community Approach.* New York: Methuen.

Nelson, Arthur C., Rolf Rendall, Casey J. Dawkins, and Gerrit J. Knapp. 2002. *The Link Between Growth Management and Housing Affordability: The Academic Evidence,* The Brookings Institution Center for Urban and Metropolitan Policy. Washington, DC: The Brookings Institution.

Pendall, Rolf. 2000. Local Land Use Regulation and the Chain of Exclusion. *Journal of the American Planning Association* 66, no. 2, Spring: 125–42.

Pigou, Arthur C. 1932. *The Economics of Welfare.* Reprint, New York: Transaction Publishers, 2002.

Pitkin County Housing Authority. 2001. 2001 *Aspen/Pitkin County Housing Guidelines,* Colorado: Pitkin County Housing Authority.

_____. 2002. *The Red Book—City of Aspen/Pitkin County Housing Programs.* Aspen, Colorado: Pitkin County Housing Authority.

Provincetown Interviews. 2002. By the author. September 2002.

Randall, Alan. 1983. The Problem of Market Failure. *Natural Resources Journal* v. 23, 131–48. Reprinted in *Economics of the Environment: Selected Readings,* 3rd ed., edited by Robert Dorfman and Nancy Dorfman, 144–161. New York: Norton & Company, 1993.

Resort Municipality of Whistler. 2000. *Whistler Sustainability Symposium.* Whistler, British Columbia, Canada: Resort Municipality of Whistler.

_____. 2001 a. *Whistler Village Enhancement Strategy.* Whistler, British Columbia, Canada: Resort Municipality of Whistler.

_____. 2001 b. *Whistler Resort Community Monitoring Report 2000.* Whistler, British Columbia, Canada: Resort Municipality of Whistler.

_____. 2001 c. *Five Year Financial Plan Survey.* Vancouver, British Columbia, Canada: McIntyre & Mustel.

_____. 2002. History, May. http://www.whistler.com/community/history/.

_____. 2003 a. *Comprehensive Backgrounder.* Whistler, British Columbia, Canada: Resort Municipality of Whistler.

_____. 2003 b. Quarterly Report, Second Quarter 2003. Whistler, British Columbia, Canada: Resort Municipality of Whistler.

Rose, Louis. 1989. Topographical Constraints and Urban Land Supply Indexes. *Journal of Urban Economics* 26, no. 3: 335–47.

Ryan, John. 2001. *Martha's Vineyard Housing Needs Assessment.* Amherst, Massachusetts: Development Cycles.

Sabatini, Joshua. 2001. Houses on Move Auction Raises $200,000 to Ease Housing Crisis. *Martha's Vineyard (MA) Gazette,* August 7. http://www.mvgazette.com/news/2001/08/07/houses_on_move_auction.php.

Samu, Dana. 2000. *Overview 2000,* The Whistler Housing Authority. Whistler, British Columbia.

_____. 2002. *Overview 2002,* The Whistler Housing Authority. Whistler, British Columbia.

Samuelson, Paul A. 1954. The Pure Theory of Public Expenditure. *The Review of Economics and Statistics* 36, no. 4: 387–89.

Schneider, Paul. 2000. *The Enduring Shore: A History of Cape Cod, Martha's Vineyard, and Nantucket.* New York: Henry Holt and Company, LLC.

Shucksmith, Mark. 1981. *No Homes For Locals?* Westmead, Farnborough, Hampshire, England: Gower Publishing Company, Ltd.

Sigelman, Nelson. 2000. In Aspen, Colorado Affordability Is a Familiar Problem. *Martha's Vineyard (MA) Times,* May 9. http://www.mvtimes.com/.

Smith, Adam. 1776 a. *The Wealth of Nations: Books I–III.* Reprint, Harmondsworth, Middlesex, England: Penguin Books, 1999.

_____. 1776 b. *The Wealth of Nations: Books IV–V.* Reprint, Harmondsworth, Middlesex, England: Penguin Books, 1999.

Stake, Robert E. 1978. The Case Study Method in Social Inquiry. *Educational Researcher 7* (February): 5–8. Reprinted in *Case Study Method,* edited by Roger Gomm, Martyn Hamersley, and Peter Foster, 19–26. Thousand Oaks, California: Sage Publications, 2000.

_____. 1995. *The Art of Case Study Research.* Thousand Oaks, California: Sage Publications.

Statistics Canada. 1996. 1996 Community Profiles. http://ceps.statcan.ca/english/Profil/PlaceSearchForm1.cfm (accessed 15/04/2003).

_____. 2001 a. 2001 Census of Canada. http://www.statcan.ca/start.html (accessed 15/04/2003).

_____. 2001 b. 2001 Community Profiles. http://www12.statcan.ca/english/profil01/Details/details1.cfm?SEARCH=BEGINS&ID=12435&PSGC=59&SGC=5931020&DataType=1&LANG=E&Province=10&PlaceName=Whistler&CMA=000&CSDNAME=Whistler&A=&TypeNamE=District%20Municipality&Prov= (accessed 15/04/2003).

Strauss, Anselm, and Juliet Corbin. 1998. *Basics of Qualitative Research,* 2nd ed. Thousand Oaks, California: Sage Publications.

Talamo, John. 1986. *The Real Estate Dictionary,* 4th ed. Boston: Financial Publishing Company.

Town of Provincetown. 1999. *1999 Annual Town Report.* http://www.provincetowngov.org/twn_rpt/99trweb/99tr.html (accessed 09/05/2002).

_____. 2002. *Affordable Housing 2002.* http://www.provincetowngov.org/affordable/affhsgindex.htm (accessed 14/08/2002).

U.S. Census Bureau. 1990. *1990 United States Census.* http://homer.ssd.census.gov/cdrom/lookup/CMD=LIST/DB=C90STF3A/LEV=STATE (accessed 12/26/2002).

_____. 1997. *1997 Economic Census.* http://www.census.gov/epcd/ec97zip/us/US00000.HTM (accessed 3/23/2004).

_____. 2000 a. http://www.census.gov/prod/cen2000/doc/ProfilesTD.pdf.

_____. 2000 b. 2000 United States Census. http://www.census.gov/main/www/cen2000.html (accessed 12/26/2002).

_____. 2000 c. *2000 County Business Patterns* NAICS. http://censtats.census.gov/cbpnaic/cbpnaic.shtml.

_____. 2002. *Demographic Profiles, United States Census 2000.* http://www.census. gov/Press-Release/www/2002/demoprofiles.html (accessed 26/12/2002).

Urquhart, Janet. 2002. Aspen wants a new look for housing. *The Aspen (CO) Times,*March 6, 2002. http://www.aspentimes.com.

_____. 2002. How many more units is enough? *The Aspen (CO) Times,* March 6, 2002. http://www.aspentimes.com.

Vineyard Housing Office. 2002. Dukes County Regional Housing Authority. http:://www.vho.vineyard.net/DCRHA.html (accessed 13/05/2002).

Whistler Housing Authority. 2002. http://www.whistlerhousing.ca/(accessed 30/04/2002).

Whistler Interviews. 2002. By the author. July 2002.

Whistler Question. 2004. http://www.whistlerquestion.com/.

Yin, *Robert K. 1994. Case Study Research, Design and Methods,* 2nd ed. Thousand Oaks, California: Sage Publications.

Index

- A -

Affordable housing, defined, 191
Analytic generalization, 22, 185, 190
Aspen, 16, 21-22, 25-27, 111-127, 186
Aspen Institute, 113
Aspen Music Festival, 113
Average family affordability, 134
Axial coding, 189

- B -

Bator, Francis, 87-89, 95
Bays of Huatulco, 17
Bed Unit, defined, 136
Bosselman, Fred, 113
Brazilian workers, 154
Building codes, 92
Bourne, Larry, 97

- C -

Cancun, 17
Cape Cod, 15-18, 149, 167
Case study research, 22, 183-185
Community, defined, 191
Community buy-in, 75-76
Community evaluation, defined, 34
Community Evaluation and Intervention Process
    Applications of, 34
    Defined, 33, 35
Community intervention, defined, 59
Community monitoring, defined, 70
Community will, 55, 75
Corbin, Juliet, 189
Critical success factors, 65, 75
Czech Republic workers, 172

- D -

Day trippers, 152, 154, 170
Deed, defined, 191
Deed restrictions, 29, 123, 143, 161
    Defined, 191
Disney World, 90

- E -

East Indian workers, 133
Environmental regulations, 93-
    94, 134
    Air quality, 94
    Fresh water, 94, 134
    Sanitation, 94, 134
Explanation building technique,
    24, 189-190
Extended stay tourists, 152, 154,
    170
External economies, defined 94
Externality, defined, 191
Externalities
    As a cause of market failure,
    31, 89, 106, 116, 134, 155, 172
    Defined, 89
    Environmental regulations,
    93
    Growth management
    regulations, 23, 31, 93, 104,
    106, 116-117, 133-134, 136, 155,
    172, 175
    Growth limits, 93
    In tourism communities, 191
    Land-use regulations, 23, 31,
    91-92, 104, 106, 116, 155, 172

Second home demand, 23,
    31, 80, 94-95, 106, 116, 133-134,
    155, 172, 175
    Supply and demand effect,
    23, 91-97
    Topographic constraints, 24,
    31, 93-94, 106, 133-134, 137, 172,
    175
    Visual impact restrictions, 92
    Zoning regulations, 23, 31, 91-
    92, 104, 106, 116, 134, 155

- F -

Free-Market Housing, 131, 157
    Defined, 113
Financing Programs 28, 70, 72
    Government sponsored, 28
    Private, 28
Funding, 75, 77, 80, 123, 143, 162,
    178

- G -

Gallent, Nick, 94
Gap analysis, 63-65, 70
Green, Richard, 91
Growth management regulation
    externality, 23, 92, 103, 116,
    134, 155, 172, 175

- H -

Hahushek, Eric, 91
Height restrictions, 92
Hilton Head Island, 17
Hispanic workers, 114

Housing affordability, measures of, 23, 40, 116-118, 134-135, 155, 172-174
Housing crisis, defined, 99, 192
Housing goal definition process, 62
Housing interventions
Effect of, 26, 121-122, 140-141, 161-162, 177-178
Changes to regulations, 161
Government mandate, 25, 176, 182
Monitoring, 70-74, 81
Planning, 25, 65-66, 120-121, 139, 178
Programs, 27-29, 80, 123, 141-143, 162-163, 178-179
Public enablement, 25, 104, 142, 161, 178
Public housing development, 25, 104, 123, 142, 161
Reaction to crisis, 25, 120-121, 159
Theory of, 31, 104, 106
Success of, 127, 147, 166, 182
Worker supply, 25
Housing resources, 63
Housing unit, defined, 192
Housing vision, 59, 75, 76

- I -

Impact Fees, 28, 142
Indicators 36-48
Community quality, 46
Demographic, 47
Housing, 36-37

Housing affordability, 38
Percentage of second homes, 39-40
Quantitative, 36
Informal community leaders, 55, 76

- J -

Jamaican workers, 172

- K -

Katz, Lawrence, 92
Key informants, 187
Key West, 17
Keynes, John Maynard, 87-88

- L -

Lake District, 17
Land, 75, 78
Land Bank, 28, 78, 143
Land-use regulation externality, 23, 92, 102, 116, 133, 155, 172

- M -

Macro trends, 48-50
Malpezzi, Stephen, 91
Market elasticity, 99-100, 155, 172
Market Failure
Defined, 90
From externalities, 23, 24, 89-95, 120, 138, 158, 175
Martha's Vineyard, 16, 21-22, 25-27, 149-165, 186

Mayflower, 167
McCarthy, Claire, 113
Median family affordability, 40,
    116, 155, 174
Micro Trends, 48-50
Mitigation, 28, 123

- O -

Oaxaca, Mexico, 17
Open coding, 189
Orlando, 17, 90
Organizational capacity, 75, 78

- P -

Pareto Optimality, 88-90
Pendall, Rolf, 92
Peterson, Craig, 113
Pigou, Arthur, 87-88
Political buy-in, 75-76
Political leaders, 54, 76
Political will, 54, 75
Price resale caps, 29, 123, 143
Provincetown, 21-22, 26-27, 167-
    182, 186
Puerto Adventuras, 17

- Q -

Quigley, John, 91

- R -

Ratio of house prices to
    household income 23, 40, 116,
    134, 155, 172

Real estate transfer tax, 28, 123
Regulatory Constraints
    Defined, 50
    Examples, 51
    Effects, 101-103
Rental subsidy, 28
Resident-restricted housing, 131,
    140-141
Resource analysis, 63-65, 70, 72
Rosen, Kenneth, 92

-S -

Sales tax, 123
Samuelson, Paul, 87-88
St. Andrews, NB, 17
Second home, defined, 192
Second home demand
    externality, 23, 80, 94-95, 116,
    134, 155, 158, 172
Selective coding, 189
Semi-structured interview
    technique, 187
Shucksmith, Mark, 93-94
Smith, Adam, 85-87
Social development theory, 90
Straus, Anselm, 189
Stellwagen Bank, 168

- T -

Tewdwr-Jones, Mark, 94
Topographic Constraints
    Defined, 53
    Examples, 53, 136
    Effects, 104

Topographic constraint
externality, 24, 93-94, 106,
133-134, 172, 175
Tourism, defined, 192
Tourism businesses, 22, 170
Tourism community, defined, 192
Tourism employment, 22, 43, 114,
132-133, 152
Tourism employment Wages, 45
Tourism workers,
Locals, 107, 114, 133, 154
Managers, 108, 114, 133, 154
New immigrants, 107, 114,
133, 154
Seekers, 107, 114, 133, 154
Triangulation, defined, 187

- U -

Undocumented workers, 114

- V -

Visioning process, 61

- W -

Warm bed policy, 147
Defined, 139
Whistler, 21-22, 25, 129-147, 186

- Y -

Yin, Robert, 183

- Z -

Zoning regulation externality, 23,
92, 102, 116, 134, 155, 172

If you enjoyed this book and would like to pass one on to someone else, please check with your local bookstore, online bookseller, or use this form:

Name_____

Address _____

City _____ State_____ Zip_____

Please send me:

_____ copies of *Living in Paradise* at $21.95 $ _____

Connecticut residents please add sales tax $ _____

Shipping*: $4.00 for the first copy and $2.00
for each additional copy $ _____

Total enclosed $ _____

Send order to:
The Wyndham Financial Group
274 Ballamahack Road
Windham, CT 06280
USA

or visit our website at www.wyndhamfinancial.com

or call   1-866-956-4477 (toll-free in the United States)
          1-860-456-4477 (worldwide)

For more than 5 copies, please contact the publisher for multiple copy rates.

*International shipping costs extra. If shipping to a destination outside the United States, please contact the publisher for rates to your location.